Erik Miteus

An unintended comedy in 3 diminishing acts.

Erik Miteus

An unintended comedy in 3 diminishing acts.

A JP Homer Classic

by J.D. Peterson

Aventine Press

First Edition

Published by Aventine Press
1023 4th Ave #204
San Diego CA, 92101
www.aventinepress.com

ISBN: 1-59330-524-9
Library of Congress: 2008920524

Printed in the United States of America

Preface: J.P. Homer's Studies in Absurdity

Since the publication of J.P. Homer's The Thesoddy, there has been a lot of interest in seeing other works of J.P. Homer, more about the adventures of Thesod, the planet Orn, and, most importantly, more about the strange green creatures known as dar mofts. All I can say is be careful what you ask for. Homer's tales should always be read with care, lest they change your view of the world in strange and unpredictable ways. –JD Peterson

The tiny planet Orn, hidden in a corner of our (or some other) universe, is a subject of debate among some of Earth's xenohistorians. We know that Ornians have visited Earth for thousands of years, exchanging tales with a few of our most famous early historians as well as with more contemporary writers. Sophocles himself said, *"One word frees us of all the weight and pain of life: that word is Orn.* And Groucho Marx mused, *"Well, Orn is Orn, isn't it? Still, on the other hand, water is water. And east is east and west is west and if you take cranberries and stew them like applesauce they taste much more like prunes than rhubarb does."* Of course, these quotes have been changed by those who either didn't hear them correctly or don't believe in Orn.

The most well known Ornian historian, J.P. Homer, lived from 2148-2026 BE (Before Enlightenment, approximately Earth's 14,516 BC), and he has an impressive 2,027 histories and historical plays attributed to him. Although human, J.P. Homer was orphaned at an early age and raised by a breed of silly, green, large-nosed humanoids known as dar mofts. This strange upbringing apparently had a great effect upon his writings and undoubtedly shaped the philosophy with which he founded the *School of Lesser Historians* when he was just 12 years old. (*He named this school George, after the uncle he never had.*)

Unfortunately, very few of J.P. Homer's works have been discovered, and generally, they have been discovered in rather nasty states, usually lining old trunks, wrapped around fish, on the bottoms of bird cages, or moldering in vaults of obscure museums. Homer's earliest discovered "birdcage" work is **The Thesoddy** (published on Earth in 2006), the tale of an epic and unnecessary voyage by Thesod of Freeny to save his country from the wrath of the gods. Since then his "trunk-work", **The Big Pang Theory of the Creating of the Universe**, and the "Fish-work", **The Creating of the Gods and Man** (2046 BE), have been found, chronicling Homer's beliefs of how Orn, its gods, and its people were created. A recent dig in a landfill in the plains of Nebraska has also found the long lost **Frankenmoft**, mummified in a wrapping of old banana peels, and newspapers from the 1920's. Preliminary translation suggests that it may reveal the origin of the very first dar moft.

At the age of 116, with his School of Lesser Historians having failed to ever recruit any students, Homer was forced to get a job as the Court Historian of Nartha (Planetary Capital of Orn). This job ended as quickly as it began, as Homer chose to write about the events precipitating the King's failed Continental War I in 2036 BE. Homer decided that the King had decided to go to war because he had eaten some particularly bad Gorf-pea stew. Homer entitled this work, appropriately enough, **War and Peas** (2032 BE). He worked in Nartha for just one month and was forced to leave rapidly (many believe without his shoes).

Artistically satisfied, yet penniless (and perhaps shoeless), Homer returned to George for his last years of life. It was during this time that George took on its first students, inspiring Homer to move into a new form of literature. He decided to devote his talents to the writing of plays, his first including **A Dinghy Named Desire** (2031 BE), **The Philosophy of Neeste** (2030 BE), **The Guy Who Liked to Look at Himself** (2028 BE), and **Erikus Miteus** (2027 BE). These plays of J.P. Homer are as diverse as they are strangely written, however they are fine examples of Lesser Histories at their most humorous. This is amusing (if not sad), since many historians suspect that Homer's plays were serious attempts in his old age at writing moving character studies.

Without the original text of these plays, it is difficult to determine what Homer was trying to say, and unfortunately none of these plays, nor his unseen final play, **The Gods Smell Badly**, have been read by anyone alive today. (*This final work was said to be his greatest . . . had it ever been read. However, the angered gods turned him into a newt and destroyed his masterwork with a lightning bolt. It remains to be determined whether Homer continued to write as a newt.*) We have to rely on sparse references by even sparser historians of his day to help us to understand J.P. Homer. Recently, however, one of his later plays, **Erik Miteus**, was discovered (encased in concrete on the bottom of Lake Michigan) in surprisingly good condition. Months of translating the ancient Ornian writing has revealed yet another serious attempt at a character study.

Erik the Mighty, famed for his youthful role helping Jasod find the Golden Fleas, finds himself crazed and despondent from being lost at sea for 30 years. He returns home to his farm, wife, and family after having failed to fight (or even find) the Ghast Garlic Wars in the faraway land of Toorelia. Once home, he fights with the many imaginary forces of evil in his wheat, kitchen tools, barn, and family at the bidding of a crazy garlic addict who wants revenge for something a different Erik did during the Ghast Garlic Wars. Interestingly, some aspects of this tale are undoubtedly autobiographical since Homer fought with his own garlic addiction for his whole life, if not longer. Although, this tale was obviously intended to probe the pitfalls of a man's preoccupation with hero fantasies, in the manner seen in the Earth classic *Don Quixote*, **Erik Miteus** ends up as cow-wrestling slap-stick and tilting at wheat-fields. Yet, for some inexplicable reason, the tale is well worth reading, if perhaps only as a study in absurdity.

J.D. Peterson

Contents

Cast of Characters

Erik the Mighty:	Erik Miteus, Captain of the Sea Leach, famed for his part in the search for the lost "Golden Fleas" in his youth. He was lost for 30 years while looking for battle in the country of Toorelia, site of the Ghast Garlic Wars. Now 60 years old, he returns to Lak-Lustar to his farm and his family.
Dwick:	First mate of the Sea Leach and faithful dar moft friend of Erik the Mighty, willing to follow his master to the 12 ends of Orn . . . for golden smoolies.
Yago of Oont	Old wandering vagabond and garlic addict from the wayafar land of Oont. A master of disguise.
Tenassity:	Noble wife of Erik the Mighty.
Facsimili and *Facsimily*	Twin daughters of Erik the Mighty, born the day after Erik left for the Ghast Garlic Wars.
Crontobasticon & Algimemmitoes	The watch-cows of Erik the Mighty.
Muckus:	The accountant swine of Erik the Mighty
Chorus:	Traditional group of three very large, singing black birds.
Sarcasto:	Book-maker of Lak-Lustar.
Dr. Phyzzic:	Doctor for all of Lak-Lustar.
Harry:	Son of Erik the Mighty.
Moose:	God of all the Gods.

Erik
Miteus

ACT I

Act I, Scene I

In which Erik the Mighty and Dwick return home after 30 years at sea, meet a smelly Oontian, and argue about their adventures.

Noontime. The docks of Lak-Lustar: In the background, a much abused and old sailing kree; to stage right, the back edge of a very large crowd of citizens, of whom only 5 or 6 are visible, facing off stage. They are cheering loudly and ringing bells while shrieking "Erik, Erik, Erik . . . !" At center stage stand Erik the Mighty and the green, large-nosed dar moft Dwick, carrying large duffel bags. Dwick holds a brightly-colored hand-puppet on one hand. The Chorus stands at stage left in the foreground.

CHORUS

Noontime at docks of Lak-Lustar it be.
A man does return from a long time at sea . . .
Erik the Mighty and friend, dar moft Dwick.
They're old from a journey that was not so quick,
but they are the story, this unlikely pair.
Erik's the strong one with thinning, grey hair,
and Dwick is the small moft who looks wimpy-weak.
Let us now listen and hear what they speak.

(Exit Chorus stage left.)

ERIK

Thank Moose, goodfull Dwick, we've come home at last,
safely and soundly, though not very fast.

DWICK

Thirty long years is but piffle to some.

(Aside, to puppet)
Not piffle to me, but it's piffle to some.

ERIK

What mutter you, man? Are you not at all proud?
Can you not hear the name that is shrieked by the
crowd?
I'm a hero to all though they know not my deeds.
A warrior I am. It's my fate, now. You heed.

(Erik watches the crowd proudly)
They're cheering my name and they're ringing a bell.
They know if I did it, it must have gone well.
Wait 'til they hear of my awesome exploits,
my swordplay so wondrous and un-maladroit
in Garlic Wars, ghastly and ruled by Death's hand.
On many an enemy I left my brand!

DWICK

(Sighing)
Once again, E the M. We were not there at all,
not spotting Toorelia nor reaching landfall.
We wandered quite lost on the muck-mucky seas
for thirty long years.

(Aside to puppet)
Does he have brain disease?

ERIK

(Rubbing his forehead)
Yes, yes, my good friend, I do sometimes forget.
I *wanted* to fight . . . and I'm really quite fit.
With one lousy punch I could fell a Death-bat,

but my night-sight is poor . . . uh, forget that.
Perhaps a snow-rhino, or Great Snakey Twist.
I could deck those foul beasties with blindfolded fists!

DWICK

(Reaches up to pat Erik's shoulder)
So danger avoided your big, bulky hide . . .
We searched and we wandered, afar and awide.
No sign of Toorelia, garlic, or fights.
Our most difficult chore was to sleep every night
after sleeping all day with near nothing to do.
Dangers were rare and quite less than a few.
All of the crew died at very old years
(except for young Newcome who died of bad cheer).

(He pauses, and grabs Erik's right arm.)
But the crowds do not know what we did or did not!
Perhaps they'll reward us with smoolies a lot
or silver or jewels or free flagons of ade.
Roll our dice right . . . and we've got it made!

ERIK

(Turning from the crowd)
Nay, gentle Dwick. We must be away
while the crowd is distracted by ship yonder. They
do think it is us that they cheer it so loud.
Such fine display. It makes me feel proud,
but still we must go, for my wife she does wait.
It's been thirty years, so I cannot be late.

(Enter from stage left, the red-haired Oontian named Yago. He is thin, sea-weary, and *smells of garlic. Hands clasped, with hunched posture, he steps in front of Dwick)*

YAGO

Excuse me, old sirs. I've been hearing the crowd
shrieking and chanting the name so, so loud,
of Erik the Warrior, returned on this day.
I wish to behold him. Pray tell me the way
to pass 'round that crowd there to reach his far kree.
I wish to see Erik. A fine warrior he be.

DWICK

(Grinning)
Give me five smoolies, and I will sure aid
you to find Erik . . . but, *after* I'm paid.

ERIK

(Silences Dwick with one raised hand)
Stay your slim wallet. I'm Erik. 'Tis true.
They cheer the wrong ship and the wrong captain, too.

DWICK

(Aside, to puppet)
Perhaps other captain has sense of finance
and at prospects of profit will not miss a chance.
And this guy smells garlicked. Either he's very proud
or a clove-headed, bulb-suck with head in the clouds.

ERIK

This is old Dwick, the first mate of my kree.
I'm Erik the Mighty, but who might you be?

YAGO

(Excitedly)
Erik the warrior, returned from a-sea?
Erik the warrior, are you sure you are he?

DWICK

(Stepping toward Yago, eagerly.)
Yes, he is he. For 10 smoolies he'll tell
of all our adventures. He tells them quite well.

YAGO

(Ignoring Dwick)
Did you fight in Toorelia's Ghast Garlic Wars?

ERIK

Yes.

DWICK

No.

ERIK

Yes.

DWICK

No, he forgets. He did more
than just crush Garlic heathens in southernly climes.
He explored risky waters, endured dangerous times.
And five extra smoolies will bring you the tale
of the island of cat-ladies.

(Waggling his eyebrows)

Such lovely tails!

ERIK

(Looks at Dwick, puzzled. Turns back to Yago.)
Risky waters, cat-ladies . . . well, at any rate
If you visit my homestead, I'll free inundate
your parched throat with ade and your belly with swill.
The tales will be wondrous, so come if you will.
The Homestead . . . a farmland that everyone knows,
20 miles north by the walking of crows.

YAGO

(Aside)
This is my chance. Such luck on this day!
He'll never forget me if I have my way.

(To Erik and Dwick)
Thank you, good sirs. I'll come some fine eve.
Remember me . . . Yago . . . & don't call me Steve.

(Exit Yago, stage *left)*

ERIK

(Angrily)
Dwick, what's this piffle of cat-ladies tails?

DWICK

Let us capitalize on some capital tales.

ERIK

(Angrily.)
You mean capitalize on some capital lies.
I'll not dress up tales in some pretty disguise
when the truth can't be beaten by anyone's dreams.
What of my fighting the troops at Careens
to save a young maiden from Purple Knight's hands?
I'll not tell your lies when the truth is so grand!

DWICK

(Shakes his head.)
That's from a book that you read for ten years,
the *Warrior Klaus Stalvart of Vegotnofears*.

ERIK

Well, what of my fine single-handed success
at smashing the army of Herman the Hess?

DWICK

(Yawning)
One Thousand and Two Pomeranian Knights
by the mad Pommer Abhul von Achtul the White.

ERIK

The Head of the Gargle?

DWICK

(Absently)
By George Baldy Smith.

ERIK

The Feather for Hairless?

DWICK

(Looks at puppet)

Eustashian myth.

ERIK

(Sputtering)
I fought off foul natives on Island of Rook,
alone against hundreds. That's not from a book.

DWICK

(Bored)
You fought against farmers . . . and they were unarmed.
We're lucky that none of those people were harmed.

ERIK

(Shrugs)
A simple mistake. They looked awful tough.
Ah, now I remember a tale good enough,
a tale you can't twist up to make me the fool.
Remember the Giant I gallantly dueled?
The people of Glin were so pleased after fight
that they followed me 'round until falling of night.

DWICK

(Suddenly smiling)
I must admit that you have me well beat.
The fight with the giant *was* a brave feat.

(Aside, to puppet)
I haven't the heart to correct this charade.
The giant he fought was just part of parade,
a great big balloon in the shape of their boss.
And when Erik popped it, the people were cross.

If we tell lies, we must have them believed.
If we talk of Toorelia, they'll know we deceive.
And stories from books will just not pass the test.
Complete, outright lying would really be best.
But this tale will pass and perhaps will amaze.
They won't know that Erik is mightily crazed.

ERIK

(Impatiently)
Enough mutters now, Mr. Dwick. Let's go home.
This hero needs some long rest from his roams.
I've many more tales for the telling to tell.
If you can't remember them . . . you are not well.

DWICK

(Aside to puppet)
His head's full of mustard, one die short of craps,
so I'd best take him home now to take a long nap.

ERIK

Stop muttering, Dwickus, and let's be away.
We can't just stand here telling stories all day!

(Exit Erik the Mighty with Dwick, hoisting their sacks. Dwick continues muttering to his puppet as they exit stage left. Enter the Chorus, gazing after them.)

CHORUS

So Erik the Mighty and sidekick named Dwick
avoided the crowds here, so loud and so thick
and wandered off home to the north and the south
(Dwick never ceasing his muttering mouth).
Erik walked proudly, his old muscles strained,
eating the miles underfoot uncomplained.

Act I, Scene II

In which Erik and Dwick, after insulting the cows, ponder the sanity of Erik's wife and daughter.

Late Mid-day. Outside the homestead of Erik the Mighty: In the center, the large farmhouse, extending across and off the stage to the left. There is a big front porch. At stage left is a fence, with a gate, where Erik and Dwick are standing. The very old cows, Crontobasticon and Algimemmitoes, stand upright on their hind legs guarding the property.

CRONTOBASTICON

(Squinting in bovine suspicion)
Looksee yon, Algi, some trespassing types.

ALGIMEMMITOES

(Calling to Erik and Dwick)
Now see here, old fellows, we're not cows to gripe,
but you've got no right to be scoping our land.
There's nobody home, so go pound some sand
or suffer a mouthful of hoofish-type taste.
You still have your teeth. It would be a waste.

CRONTOBASTICON

(Raising one hoof threateningly)
Be off with ye, scurvies, no meals for ye here.
And don't look at our grass, if ye hold yer life dear.
Just take yer foul little opposable thumbs
and fly like the wind takes up dried-out bread-crumbs.

ERIK

Don't you remember? You were but a calf
when we left years ago, twenty-nine and two halfs.
Algi, I'm Erik, and this, good old Dwick!
Look at us, cows, has your milk become thick?!

CRONTOBASTICON

(Frowns cowishly)
I recall Erik as much younger man,
about an inch taller with less of a tan.
Yer much, much too old to be Erik. I'm sure
that if ye get help there must be a cure.

ERIK

(Pounds one mighty fist on the fence post)
I'm Erik, I tell you! I'm older of course.
Are you really Cronto . . . or a quite ugly horse?

ALGIMEMMITOES

See here old man. There's just no excuse
for laying out such un-cowlike abuse.

ERIK

(Turning away)
You're udderly senile. I've had enough.
I raised you myself and you now give me guff.

ALGIMEMMITOES

If you're truly Erik, you'd have no thick beard,
you'd have scar on your cheek, a birthmark quite weird,
bluish-grey eye-bags, and muscles quite hard.

ERIK

(Triumphant)
Will this do, old Algi . . . my library card?

(Erik shows Algimemmitoes his library card, while the cow squints suspiciously.)

(Enter the pig, Muckus, from stage right, walking spryly upon his hind legs.)

MUCKUS

(Happily)
Algimemmitoes, Cronto, what are they doing here?
Erik and Dwick were gone many a year.
Don't leave them standing there hoisting their sacks.
Let them in cow-girls and cease your attacks.

(Aside to Erik and Dwick.)
They haven't the manners of pigs, I'm afraid.
Too many buckets of butter they've made,
perhaps leaving butter on old bovine brains.
They'll start thinking better if we have some rain.

(Muckus hugs Erik warmly, snuffling swinishly.)

DWICK

Thanks, good pig Muckus, you old, faithful swine.
Now out of my way, cows. I'm feeling un-fine.
I must go inside, now we've ended turmoil,
to quick relieve bladder . . . 'fore breeches are soiled.

(Exit Dwick, running, and Muckus, walking, into the farmhouse.)
(Enter the elderly and beautiful Tenassity from stage right.)

TENASSITY

Erik!

ERIK

Tenassity!

TENASSITY

Erik, my love!

ERIK

I've missed you my darling, my featherless dove.

(Erik and Tenassity embrace passionately and kiss, a long kiss.)

CRONTOBASTICON

(Whispering to Algimemmitoes)
She kisses this man, and gods know where he's been.
He is not the prettiest nor cleanest of men.
Muck says he's Erik, but I'm still unsure
of this man with the muscle-bound, bulky figure.
For one thing this man-thing is much, much too old.
A little bit older he'd push up the mold!

(Erik and Tenassity are still kissing.)

ALGIMEMMITOES

(Whispering to Crontobasticon)
A little bit younger and he'd still be quite aged.
This cannot be Erik. Let's cease this outrage!

(Erik and Tenassity are still kissing.)

CRONTOBASTICON

(To Algimemmitoes)
But what if it is? We could be all wrong.
Accusing him wrongly could be our swan-song.
We must play this safely. We'll watch him well
to discover the truth here that causes bad smells.

(Exit cows, stage right. Erik and Tenassity return to the land of the non-kissing.)

TENASSITY

Erik, my only, my favorite pastime
why didn't you call me. Had you no dime?
I waited and waited, but still you were gone.
Many years passed here, so slow . . . on and on.
I happen to know that you weren't at the fight.
Where were you, Erik? Why didn't you write?

ERIK

I did write, my Tenny. I wrote every day.
But I couldn't find Post Offices so far away.

(Erik empties his large sack onto the ground. It's all letters, hundreds. Tenassity picks up a couple and reads.)

TENASSITY

(Reading)
"My dearest Tenny, I'm lost out at sea.
Hope you are well and hope you miss me."

(Tenassity reads another letter.)
"Dearest, my Tenny, I'm still lost at sea.
Hope you are well and still missing me."

They're very nice letters, my husbandly love.
I'm just glad that you're home, my big, hairy dove.

(Pauses, musing)
In town of Lak-Lustar what strange day this be.
Two mighty warriors returned from the sea.
Erik the Blue today also came back.

ERIK

He had not the welcome we got. That's a fact!

(Looks toward the farmhouse)
Now where's our son, Harry? Is he not here?
When I had left he was more than one year.

TENASSITY

Harry's away at the market in Flay
selling some hay. He'll be back in five days,
but you must meet Facsimili, Facsimily, too.

(Turns to the farmhouse)
Facsimili, Facsimily! You'll never guess who
has arrived on our porchstep so many years late!
You come out here now! Don't make father wait!

(Enter Facsimili from the farmhouse door. She is tall and slender, with long black hair, and she wears a long, red dress and an apron. Dwick follows behind her.)

TENASSITY

Erik. Facsimili. She was born aft you sailed.
Did you receive notice? Did you get my mail?

DWICK

Yes, we received notice one day out to sea.

(Aside, to puppet)
Or did we? My 30 year memory fails me.
He did get the letter. I read the first line
to Erik as we began journey so fine.
"Your wife did give birth," then a wet gale blew strong,
taking the letter, full three pages long.

(Dwick shrugs)

FACSIMILI

Daddy, oh Daddy! We've missed you so much.
You really should learn to keep better in touch!

(Facsimili hugs her father joyously.)

ERIK

(To Tenassity)
She's a beautiful daughter we have standing here!

TENASSITY

She's pretty as Facsimily inside, the good dear,
who's busy preparing the night's dinner feast.

ERIK

(Puzzled)
Whether outside or inside, no difference the least.

She's mannered and nice . . . and really unloud.
Facsimili's fine, and she makes father proud.

TENASSITY

Go inside, Facsimili. Bring Erik fresh clothes.
Tell Facsimily to bring swill. First course, I suppose.

(Facsimili joyously hugs her father once more and then exits into the farmhouse. Erik and Tenassity sit on the porch. Dwick sits on the steps.)

DWICK

(Yells after Facsimili.)
And swill for me, too! And fresh jerkin to boot!

(Aside to puppet.)
She did not hear me at all . . . hairless newt!

ERIK

(To Tenassity)
Fresh clothes and a meal. She works like she's two.
It's no wonder she tells herself what chores to do!

TENASSITY

(Laughing, she kisses Erik.)
You are so funny. Like two, do you say?
I must tell Facsimili and Facsimily the way
you joke with me, Erik. It shames me they've never
known of your humor that's always so clever.

(Exit Tenassity into the farmhouse.)

ERIK

"They"? My wife's crackers! She thinks there are two!
What is a sane, mighty warrior to do?
She has rats in her belfry, her marbles are gone.

DWICK

A screw loose, unbalanced. She's off, she's not on.

ERIK

I must tell her gently. Facsimili's but one.

DWICK

Blown top, off her rocker . . . her brain is undone.

ERIK

The pressures of son-ing and daughter-ing alone . . . .

DWICK

Shatter-brained, brain-sick, tetched, cuckoo's flown.

ERIK

I hope I can cure her, no docs . . . unassisted.

DWICK

She's bughouse, she's balmy, neurotic . . . she's twisted.

(Erik glares at Dwick)

ERIK

Cut the dung, Dwicky! I've had quite enough.

DWICK

(Aside to puppet)
Obsessive, compulsive, she's plain off her snuff.

(Exit Dwick, stage right. Enter Facsimily (identical twin of Facsimili) wearing a long, green dress. She carries a tray of swill.)

FACSIMILY

Father, oh father. I'd never have thought
that I'd ever see you. I missed you alot!

(Facsimily sets down the tray of swill and hugs Erik.)

ERIK

(Confused)
It hasn't been long, girl, but I love you, too.
Please join me in dining . . . and mother. Please do.
I'll tell you both tales of the frenzied, wild sea,

(Pauses, sadly)
. . . though not a thing actually happened to me.
Your dad must tell true of the last 30 years.
There was not much to see and not much to hear,
but I did see some critters that looked really strange
as we traveled vast distance upon the sea range.
Truth it be known that your dad is a dweeb
and took the wrong turning just outside of Queebs.

FACSIMILY

(Hugging her father again)
Oh father, you're home and a hero to me
whatever the tale that you tell us may be.
But please wait to tell us until later on
when all may be here & we'll listen 'til dawn.

(Exit Facsimily into the farmhouse.)

ERIK

She talked of herself as if she was not here.
Something is odd. Something is queer.
I feel very bad now . . . away for so long
that both mother and daughter became "headed" wrong.
I must make amends. Yes, I must make things well.
They'll feel better when later they hear tales I tell.

(Erik begins eating his swill. The Chorus enters.)

CHORUS

Erik the Mighty sat eating his swill,
dining emphatically . . . eating his fill.
But he sat sadly and mused while he ate,
wondering if it was family fate
for his wife and his daughter to be muchly crazed.
Erik the Mighty did feel a bit dazed.

Soon the sun falls until just a bit shows
making long Erik-the-Mighty shadows.
And Erik then enters his farmhouse so bright
and readies himself to tell tales all the night.

Act I, Scene III

In which Erik tells of his adventures while the others mutter among themselves.
Evening time. Inside the farmhouse of Erik the Mighty: In the center of the room is an enormous fireplace and hearth. Erik sits in a large chair with Tenassity at his side.

(Enter Facsimili, wearing a red dress, from stage left.)

FACSIMILI

Mother, the dishes are clean and away.
Is there more to be done before ending the day?

TENASSITY

Nothing, good daughter. Is Facsimily through
doing the laundry? She may need you.
But after you're done, come you both back in here,
for father has tellings a-plenty to hear.

(Exit Facsimili, stage left.)
(Enter Facsimily, wearing a green dress, from stage right.)

FACSIMILY

Mother and Father, I'm still washing clothes
and when I can finish them, nobody knows.
Pray tell Facsimili her hands I don't need
in doing this tedious laundry-ous deed.
And don't wait for me, father. Start your fine yarns.
I'll hear them later. But for now . . . to the barn.

ERIK

We have many a year to make up lost decades,
so do all your chores. My tales will not fade.

(Exit Facsimily, stage right.)

ERIK

(Puzzled)
Was she not just wearing red moments back?

TENASSITY

Facsimili wears red.

ERIK

I saw green. That's a fact.

TENASSITY

Facsimily wears green.

ERIK

Well, make up your mind!

TENASSITY

I'm not understanding the problem you find.

ERIK

(Sadly)
Then never you mind. Let me start on my tales.

Dwick, Algi, Cronto! Come dragging your tails!
I'm starting my stories . . . and bring Muckus, too!

TENASSITY

Facsimili wishes to also hear you.

ERIK

But Facsimili's busy with chores, is she not?

TENASSITY

Facsimily's busy. Facsimili's not.

(Erik looks at Tenassity sadly.)

ERIK

My dove, there is something of which I must speak.

TENASSITY

Then speak of it, Erik. Your voice is not weak.

ERIK

Tenny, there's but only one . . .

(Enter Dwick, Crontobasticon, Algimemmitoes, Muckus, and Facsimili from stage left, interrupting very loudly.)

DWICK

Let us go!!!!!
We are all ready to start up this show!!!
Tales full of danger and noble, good deeds.
Listen to Erik and his wisdom heed.

For just three small smoolies from each, every one
I'll tell you the tale of our trip to the sun,
as soon as he's finished. It's really quite good.
We had to wear thick gloves and fire-proof hoods

ERIK

(Shaking his head)
Sit yourself down, Dwick. There's no profit here
to be gained from my wonderful family so dear.
Let's roll the ball, get the road on the show.
I'll tell you things that you never could know.

MUCKUS

I'm so excited, my muzzle is wet.
It will be much fun . . . I'm willing to bet.

(Algimemmitoes and Crontobasticon whisper to each other.)

CRONTOBASTICON

(To Algimemmitoes)
This is our chance to now hear the man slip,
revealing his true name and letting hand tip
his base, hidden plans. We must listen well
to pile up our proof and Tenassity tell.

ALGIMEMMITOES

(To Crontobasticon)
And I brought some parchment for us on this night
to write down his story . . . but I cannot write.

(There is a loud knock on the front door.)

FACSIMILI

Perhaps now already Facsimily's done.

TENASSITY

Why would she knock?

ERIK

(Gestures to Facsimili)

How could she knock, hon?
It must be a neighbor just come to our door,
eager to hear of my traveling lore.

(Erik answers the door and finds Yago standing on the porch.)

ERIK

Come on in, Bob.

YAGO

I am Yago at hand.
I'm hoping your offer for stories still stands.
We met on the docks. You offered me food.
I trust you remember. I hope I'm not rude.

ERIK

Come in then, Dobby.

YAGO

It's Yago, my friend.

ERIK

Yobbo or Nob . . . it's the same in the end.
No man's a peninsula, free on 3 sides,
unless he is trying real hardly to hide.

Bog, meet Tenassity, love-lovely wife,
Dwick, my friend I have known my whole life,
Facsimili, born while I sailed far away.
Cronto and Algi, my cows with backs swayed,
and Muckus, my fine pig with brain quite unsmall.

YAGO

(Slyly)
I am quite pleased to be meeting you all.

TENASSITY

(To Facsimili)
Dearie, get swill for this scruffy, fine gent.
Show Quickslivver goodly intentions are meant
for wandering strangers appeared at our door.
Bring him his fill . . . and then bring him more.

(Exit Facsimili stage left.)

TENASSITY

Welcome, good Snob.

YAGO

Call me Yago, do please.

TENASSITY

Well, Yoda, are you from far over seas?

YAGO

Not from far west. But not from near east.
The travel's not long, but it's not short the least.
It's not too far south, and it's not too far north.
Far enough to stay home . . . too short not to sail forth.

TENASSITY

(Politely)
It sounds to me like it's a very nice place.

DWICK

(Aside to puppet)
Sounds more like his mouth's in a very quick race
to outrun the truth of his home's true location.
He'd have us think that he's here on vacation.
And he still smells of garlic. What is at hand?
I hope he's not after the profit I've planned.

(Enter Facsimili from stage left, carrying a large bowl of swill.)

FACSIMILI

Here is swill, Bobby.

YAGO

It's Yago, my dear.

ERIK

(Interrupting)
Let's begin tales. Are you ready to hear?

MUCKUS

My muzzle's so wet now I hardly can wait.

DWICK

Yes, let's get started. It's getting quite late.

(Yago sits on the floor and begins eating his swill. The rest sit on the floor in a semi-circle around Erik's chair, waiting expectantly. The Chorus enters quietly from stage right.)

ERIK

Three decades ago began the turmoil.
War had fast come to Toorelia's soil
over the right to use garlicky root.
Much more than that, I don't know a hoot.

CHORUS

Whoever eats garlic will swagger around
getting in fights or play-acting the clown.
After whole bulb, all your brain becomes fried,
making you feel as though you have just died,
and causing delusions and visions amazed.
Basically clove-heads become muchly crazed . . .
and no one . . . nobody . . . can eat only one.
They start eating daily because it's so fun.
Saucy tomatoes they make with cloves minced
and spread them on pasta. The thought makes us wince.
For garlic bread, most men would rip out your spine
while saying, "Life's wondrous, life's spiffy, life's fine.

ERIK

(Gesturing angrily at the Chorus)
Shut your beaks, Chorus. I'm telling this tale.
One more loud chirp and I'll kick feathered tail.

(He pauses to compose himself)
The war was quite awful . . . fathers fought sons,
and sons fought with brothers. It wasn't much fun.
I guess garlic madness did many possess.
I just don't know who did start all this mess.

CHORUS

The traders from Oont brought much cargo of cloves
to Toorelia's shore through vast, hiddenly coves.
They sold garlic to children, trapping them in
a life of addiction, wasting and thin.
Crime ran the rampage as clove-heads were made,
robbing and thieving for money to trade
for just one more bulb or a small clove or two.

(Erik waves impatiently for the Chorus to be silenced.)

CHORUS

There was nothing Toorelia's people could do
but wage a tough war upon Oontian scum.
They asked help from others. They asked them to come
to rid our fair Orn of such foul, foul behavior.
They needed much help, and they needed a savior

(Erik glares at the Chorus.)

ERIK

Now, as I had said, before being disturbed,
Toorelia's problems did need to be curbed.

Who do you think they decided to ask
to fight in this war, a nast, loathesome task?
Come on, you all know! Here in front of your backs
sits Erik the Mighty. Learn all your facts!

I was a famed war hero, way, way back then,
and built like a muskox (much unlike my ken).
I've always read tales of great heroes a lot,
and had proved many times that what they had, I've got,
the wiseness of Aker, the eye-sight of Skreet,
Harry Clean's strength, and the speed of Jack Fleet.
My strength it was swordplay, and I was a champ.
At the prospect of fighting me, men became damp
in their breeches from fear and they quick ran away.

So, of course I was chosen to sail to the fray
in the land of Toorelia. Others were, too,
such as Wim, the Unkind, and brave Erik, the Blue,
Makkie, the Knife, and Big Crum, the Abused.
We each set our sails with our own crews and cruised.

CHORUS

So they sailed, & they sailed, & they sailed, & they sailed,
through wetly, wet seas while the wind howled and galed.
Until one dark night on brave Erik's *Sea Leach,*
when all of the lands were quite far out of reach,
one crew-member should have kept eyes on the sea
to make sure the ship was just where it should be,
but Erik thought Dwick was the one on the watch,
and Dwick thought the job was to be done by Botch,
and Botch thought the watch was just officer stuff,
and so on, and so on . . . .

ERIK

All right, Chorus. Enough.
Let me just say that we lost other krees
and sailed on alone on the muck-mucky seas.

YAGO

(Eagerly, watchfully)
When did you reach far Toorelia's shores,
becoming a hero in Ghast Garlic Wars?

ERIK

Soon after that.

DWICK

No. We didn't get there.
Didn't see it, nor smell it, nor hear hide or hair.

ERIK

We did.

DWICK

No we didn't.

ERIK

We did. Don't mind Dwick.
Ever since traveling he's become thick.
He forgets whole adventures, but we'll get to those.
Where was I? Oh, yes. The direction we chose
after losing the others was wrong just near Queebs,
making me feel like an idiot dweeb.

DWICK

(Aside to puppet)
I hope he forgets brave adventures from books,
or he will really appear like a schnook.
I'll never earn smoolies if tales are not bought.
I can't sell book-rights if the falsehoods are caught.
But, he's back on track. There my hope flies.
His "truths" are better than most peoples' lies.

(Yago snatches away Dwick's hand puppet and moves a short distance away.)

YAGO

(Aside to Dwick's puppet)
I do think Dwick tries to cover his tale.
I think I know what they hide. They will fail
to conceal their foul role in the Ghast Garlic War.
In the name of my Spunky, this I have swore.

ERIK

(Looks angrily at both Dwick and Yago)
Would you two rather listen, or mutter aloud?
I have a tale of which I am quite proud,
a story of chivalry, wisdom and fights.
At this slow rate it will take all the night.

CHORUS

(Helpfully)
When last you stopped you were outside of Queebs,
taking a wrong turn and feeling a dweeb.

ERIK

(Angry)
Thank you, good Chorus. Now quiet you down.
For telling this yarn I don't need you around.
Turn your tail-feathers and go out the door.
I'll not endure interruptions no more.

(Exit Chorus, huffily, stage right.)

ERIK

(Sighing)
Now as I was saying before the intrudes,
I was well lost with all my sea-dudes.
Then suddenly on the horizon ahead
was Toorelia's finely-fine, sandy beachhead.

DWICK

(Panicked)
That's not true, Erik.

ERIK

Oh, yes. Sorry Dwick.
We hadn't reached there. 'Twas the Isle of Bad Rick.
He'd kidnapped the princess . . . or was it her pig?

MUCKUS

I love pig romance. Was the sow pretty big?

ALGIMEMMITOES

Were there any bulls? A large, horny lot?

CRONTOBASTICON

(Aside to Algimemmitoes)
Don't believe this imposter. Brave Erik he's not.

YAGO

(Aside to Dwick's puppet)
They hide their war crimes by quick changing the plot.
Clever, good actors by far they are not.

ERIK

Each time I pause all this muttering starts.
Let's start again, you uncouth upstarts.

One day we sailed near suspicious, small isles,
and I ordered a stopping and watching awhile.
Well, soon enough great big warriors came out,
taunting us foully by waving sea-trout.
After some while of this fishy demeanor
I leaped overboard to show them who's meaner.
With sword in my teeth and a mind full of gore
I swam through the water and reached the near shore.

On Toorelia's beach Oonty army did wait,
and I struck up my sword to show them their fate
in the dark realm of Hatees as shambling dead.
At sight of my swordplay the whole army fled

DWICK

(Aside to puppet-less hand)
'Tis certain they ran, those poor fisher blokes.
Erik's wild fury was not any joke.
They only did offer a free meal of trout,
but Erik the Mighty did run them right out.

ERIK

(Confused, rubbing his head)
Wait. It was Munchen and not other place,
not Oontian army that ran in disgrace.
No, I fought Purple Knight over damsel's distress.
He was acting real strangely and wearing a dress.
No, Hermafrodity I think that one was.
Where was I anyway? My head's abuzz.

TENASSITY

(Concerned, stroking Erik's head)
Perhaps, Erik love, we should end for tonight
and try it tomorrow. It's late and not light.

ERIK

It has been long day. Dave, would you like to stay
in the barn with the cows, asleep in the hay?

YAGO

It's Yago. Thanks kindly, sir, for your fine bed.

(Aside to Dwick's puppet)
Though likely a hay-filled and dirty, old shed.

DWICK

(Grabs Yago's pupetted hand)
Give me my puppet, malodorous swine.

(To Muckus)
No offence, Muckus. But puppet is mine.

(Dwick snatches the puppet away from Yago and exits stage left.)

FACSIMILI

Good night, dear father.

MUCKUS

'Night, Erik. You're swell.
I hope you have more piggy stories to tell.

(Facsimili kisses Erik's cheek, and she and Muckus exit stage right.)

CRONTOBASTICON

(Suspiciously)
Good night, old stranger . . . I mean Erik the M.
I'll remember yer yarns. Every last word of them.

ALGIMEMMITOES

We will be watching like good watch-cows do.
Keeping our eyeballs and earflaps on you.

(Exit Crontobasticon and Algimemmitoes stage right. Enter Facsimily, returned from her laundry-ous deeds.)

FACSIMILY

Is storytime over? The laundry is done.
I guess I have already missed all the fun.

Good night, my dear father. We welcome you home
from your long years away in your dangerous roams.

(Facsimily kisses Erik on the cheek and exits stage right. Erik looks at her and sighs sadly.)

TENASSITY

Erik, show Yago the barn where he sleeps

ERIK

I won't be too long, Ten. Awake will you keep?
It's been many a decade away from my love.
I missed you my darling, my featherless dove.

TENASSITY

(Tenderly touches Erik's cheek)
I'll wait for you, Erik. I pray don't be long.
I've yearned for you, handsome, my husband so strong.

(Exit Tenassity stage left.)

ERIK

On to the barn, old man Boogy, my friend.
A deep pile of hay can be nice at day's end.

Act I, Scene IV

In which Yago warns Erik of warriors in the wheat, feeds the cows garlic, and plans revenge for his hamster.

Night. Inside the barn of Erik the Mighty: To stage left a large door, wide open. Four cow stalls line the wall at stage right. At the back of the stage, large piles of hay line the wall where farm tools (shears, sickles, hammers, saws, new-fangled thing from Nuyork, etc . . . .) hang on hooks. Crontobasticon and Algimemmitoes stand together on their hind legs, whispering behind concealing front hooves.

(Enter Erik and Yago from stage left. The cows stop whispering and gaze at the intruders.)

ERIK

Here we are Dobbin.

YAGO

It's Yago. I plead . . .

ERIK

No need to beg, Doggo. We'll give what you need.
You've met my old cows. No need to say names,
since when you last heard them they were much the same.
Pick any cow-stall that they do not use
and fill it with hay. Sleep you'll not lose
since the hay is spring-fresh and the cows do not snore.
A man could not ask Gods for anything more.

YAGO

(Aside, muttering)
Except decent bed and a clean room to sleep.
I'm really disliking this beefed-up old creep.

ERIK

What?

YAGO

I said I enjoyed Mighty family a lot.
That's really two finely-fine daughters you've got.

ERIK

You're wacko, good Gonno. I have only one.
She changes her clothes oft. I guess just for fun.

YAGO

(Aside, muttering)
I think he believes this! Yet some call *me* nuts.
This guy is real crazy, no ands, ifs, or buts.

ERIK

You like barns, too? You're a man of good taste,
not one to miss finer aspects in haste.
So many memories do fill this fine shack . . .
I used these here shears in a weevil attack.

(Walks over to the farm tools hung on the wall.)

Many's the harvest I've reaped here by hand,
using that sickle and getting quite tanned.
That hammer, that saw, and that hay-pitching fork,

as well as that new-fangled thing from Nuyork.
were mightily useful in working our home.
Without them we'd be in the woods on the roam.

As a young child I would come here to read
stories of battles, fine heroes and deeds.
I fancied that I am the heroely kind,
looking around for some villain to find.
I was stout Zardoz or Zorba the Geek,
exactly the opposite of anyone meek.
This barn was my world, where I fought all my fights.
Even today I feel like this barn's knight.

But enough of nostalgia. It's good to return.
"The future's an oak tree . . . the past is a fern."

(Erik turns to leave.)

YAGO

Wait, goodly Erik! I pray do hold on!

(Yago pulls Erik out of hearing of the cows.)
There is something quite urgent of which I must speak.
It's not for the wimpy, not for the weak . . . .

Only a hero can handle this news,
and you are a hero. You cannot refuse.
I sense a dark evil concealed in your wheat,
warriors with grainy-eyed heads and root-feet.
They are not wheat-plants, but armies of grain.
I've seen this before . . . thousands were slain.
You can reap havoc! You must save us all!
Harvest their little wheat-butts, or we fall!

ERIK

(Amused)
Your brain is . . . how can I say . . . jellified.

YAGO

(Solemnly)
No, look out the door. Open eyes wide.

(Yago pulls Erik toward the door and points out into the fields.)

YAGO

Cannot you see in this darkness of night?
The soldiers are watching us, waiting to fight!

(Erik peers into the dark wheat fields.)

ERIK

(Gasps)
I see wheat . . . no, I see eyes in the field . . .
and movement. It must be a cat or land seal,
but I do feel some strangeness. That I admit.
As if something or someone is here that don't fit.
The gods always test me, for they know I'm strong.

(Pause, musing)
Warriors in wheat could be what is wrong.

YAGO

You must believe, Erik. To me truth is plain,
for in a past life I was Shirley MacLaine.
If you have doubts, then another comes near,
a Wiser from Queebs, Greatest Nikey the Seer.
He has red hair like mine, and he's just the same height,

although he wears robes, and he has the thirdsight.
He's due to pass by, indeed I would say
that he's due on the morrow, quite early of day.

(Stares into the wheat field and pretends fear. He jumps.)
Yikes! Wheat moved again! Do they ready for war?

ERIK

(Angrily)
Just let them try. I'll give war . . . AND MUCH MORE!

(Pause)

But I'll wait until morning to talk to this man.
Meanwhile in case they attack us I can
sharpen my sword and then make armor shine.
I'll show those wheat-nasties. On grain we will dine.
I'LL SNAP THEIR WHEAT-BODIES AND HACK AT THEIR LEAVES,
STOMP ON THEIR ROOTS, AND THEIR TINY HEADS CLEAVE . . .

(Pause)

But . . . this assumes curses on wheat he'll assess.
Most possibly we can avoid this whole mess.
I am a peaceful and gentle, calm type . . . .
but if a foul situation comes ripe,
I'LL SLAY ME SOME PLANTS WITH MY SHARPLY-SHARP SWORD!
I'LL NEVER STOP UNTIL EACH-ALL ARE GORED!!

(Exit Erik the Mighty, stage left. The cows, continuing to stand on their hind legs, move over to talk to Yago.)

CRONTOBASTICON

Hey, you! Old man! We scorn men of yer height,
but we'll let ye sleep in the stall on the right

although ye smell strangely and look strangely, too.
Don't ye forget we've got four eyes on you!

ALGIMEMMITOES

Yes, we are cowish, suspiciously types.
One little mistake and we'll turn you to tripe.

YAGO

(Smiling, slyly)
Hold on there, cows. I . . . um . . . work for your king,
and I'm here on a spying adventure-type thing.
Yes, that's exactly what I'm here to do.
And I couldn't help overhearing you two
muttering often and gazing with ire
at Erik the Mighty as if he's a liar.

CRONTOBASTICON

(Tapping one hoof to chin, musing)
Yes, yer right, Stinky. He lies very well,
saying untruths even worse than your smell.
He is not Erik. Of this we are sure.
But awaiting for good proof we must long endure.

YAGO

Why await truths. Let us force out the lies.
Perhaps you can be my apprenticing spies.
Erik is here to take over your land
in the name of foul heathens, this ugly old man.
I have a plan that I'm sure cannot miss,
but first you both must completely eat this.

(Yago give them each an entire bulb of garlic to eat.)

ALGIMEMMITOES

(Sniffing suspiciously)
This stuff will make us smell just like you do.

YAGO

Um . . . It's also the secret to spying well, too.
How else can the king know who all his spies be?
Plus, it gives spy-powers. This stuff's the key
to seeing things others can hardly perceive,
and it keeps the king's men from being deceived.

CRONTOBASTICON

(Nods to Algimemmitoes)
Well, that's all right then. We'll chomp it right down.

ALGIMEMMITOES

Let's eat it now. No use waiting around.

(Crontobasticon and Algimemmitoes eat the garlic bulb, at least ten cloves each.)

CRONTOBASTICON

(Eyes wide)
Wow. Look at the lights. Everything's green.

ALGIMEMMITOES

(Head turning left and right)
I'm seeing things that have never been seen.
We've both been so lonely for all of these years
surrounded unknowing by beefy, bull-steers.

(Calls to imaginary beefy, bull steer.)
Come over here, honey.

CRONTOBASTICON

(Snorting)
No. That's a giraffe.
Courting that one would be quite a big laugh!

ALGIMEMMITOES

(Miffed)
He's not a giraffe. You take that back,
or I'll strike out with hooves and give you a smack.

CRONTOBASTICON

If that is yer liking, far be it for me
to ruin yer romance. Long necks and knob-knees
must be yer ideal, but I do prefer
that bull over there with the blackly, black fur.

ALGIMEMMITOES

That is a mongoose, but ten inches tall.
I think he is just a little too small.

CRONTOBASTICON

(Shaking one hoof in Algimemmitoes' face)
If I weren't so tired I'd hit yer fat nose,
but I'd rather sleep for ten years, I suppose.

ALGIMEMMITOES

(Large cow yawn)
Suddenly I'm very tired as well.
Tired, so tired . . . but don't we smell swell.

(Algimemmitoes and Crontobasticon fall into a dazed trance, now standing on all four legs rather than upright. Yago watches quietly, chewing on a clove of garlic.)

YAGO

Sleep, gentle cows. You just sleep and hear well.
You'll do all my bidding. You're under my spell

Listen, my cow-friends, and you shall now hear
the plans I have plotted these past twenty years.
He calls himself Erik, but you know the truth.
You must careful follow him like bovine sleuths
to discover his secrets and spying-type friends.
We must know his means to his horrible ends.
So eat of the garlic and follow him 'round.
Don't trust him. Don't like him. And don't make a
sound.
Report back to me all that you hear and see,
but for now fall asleep like the dumb cows you be.

(Aside to hay)
I don't wish them to hear while I soliloquize,
so let them sleep deafly and with four blind eyes.

(The cows collapse in a heap on the floor and begin snoring loudly. Yago paces angrily around the barn.)

YAGO

(Angrily pacing the barn)
Another bad lie! These cows, they do snore!
I'll show Mighty Erik! I'll settle the score!
It's quite bad enough that just 20 years back,
when I did sail upon the Big Mack,
this warrior named Erik attacked our fine kree
killing the crew, excepting for me.

The crew had been nice. We sailed choppy waves
with hold full of garlic. It was all the rave
in the land of Toorelia. We sold many cloves.
Folks came to the docks to buy it in droves.
A ship from Lak-Lustar we spied near-away,
so we fired our cannons in foul, bloody fray.
But our crew was garlicked and shooting at gulls,
and quite soon the enemy guns pierced our hull.

(Stops pacing, covers his face with his hands.)
We sank, quickly sank, and the crew . . . they all died.
If I said I cared much, you'd know that I lied,
for I only care that my nice Spunky drowned,
my love-lovely hamster so golden and brown.
Erik is evil, and he planned this all
just to kill Spunky, my rodent so small.

(Looks to the godly heavens)
Oh Spunky, my Spunky, I miss your sweet smile.
I remember the first time we met. It was while
I was lonely, so lonely and having bad times.
You came to me, Spunky, you excellent mime,
and gestured to me that you would be my friend.
Since then I'd no fears of a lone, garlicked end.
Whenever I garlicked, I'd know you'd be there,
dancing for me, the light gleaming your hair.
You carried much wisdom in two pouchie cheeks,
revealing to me all the answers I seek.

(Eyes begin to look crazed and he staggers a bit as he resumes his pacing.)

You taught me that evil's the unit of life,
that all gods are stupid, there's much fun in strife,
that lying men have very tiny ear lobes,
and that aliens from space always wear bright, blue
robes.

Why weren't you around when I wasn't bulbed out?
No one believed when I told them about
my wonderful Spunky. They all cruelly laughed,
thinking me strange . . . thinking me daft.

Spunky, oh Spunky, I do this for you,
revenge upon Erik who made your life through.
I'll punish him, Spunky. Of me you'd be proud.
The scope of my planning would leave others wowed.
First I've convinced cows that Erik's a spy,
and garlicked them out and convinced them of lies.
Second, I'm driving brave Erik insane,
getting him warring upon his own grain.
His war-guilt's so great that he's hiding his mind
among fancy stories of war-romance kind.
I'll use this guilt against this foul man.
I'll get our revenge. I know that I can!
I'll drive wife away, and his dumb children, too.
Even his piggy will change all his views.
I'll get him to burn up his very own house
and attack all his neighbors. He'll look like a louse.

(Sinks to his knees.)
Spunky, my rodent, I almost can hear
your chittering teeth, as if you are near.

My miming, brown hamster, you're my only friend.
Make all my hamsterless sufferings end!
Mimes never really die. This I do know.
They just move along to some other fine show.
Come back to me, Spunky. I need your smart brain.
I fear nights of thundering when it does rain.

(Yago rises to his feet and staggers across the barn.)

The barn starts to spin around and around,
full of the dead Big Mack crew who all drowned.

No! Stay away! Avenge your own deaths.
You keep away from me with your foul breaths.
Birds! Nasty birds! The microwave's on!
The bees in the trees are now just about gone!
Thunder and rain. Where's Spunky now
when I do most need him? I have only cows.
Sleep. I must sleep. The hay looks so soft.
I just hope the buzzards in here stay aloft.

(Yago collapses in one of the cow stalls and sleeps. Enter the Chorus.)

CHORUS

So nast Yago sleeps. His foul plans are revealed.
He has evil plots, but he's getting free meals.
He's mad and he's garlicked, a bad combination.
If we could tell Erik we'd stop altercations,
but then play would end. You'd have nothing to do.
We must let the Fates control plot through and through.
Will Yago accomplish his plans so obscene?
You'll have to continue and see the next scene.

Erik Miteus

ACT II

Act II, Scene I

In which Erik speaks to Nikey the Seer, fights with the warriors in the wheat, and protects his cows from a bookmaker.

Morning. Next to the wheat fields of Erik the Mighty: To stage left is the barn with the side and front visible, the large barn door wide open. At stage right, the edge of the large wheat field, twenty or thirty stalks of wheat are in neat rows. In the background can be seen some of the rest of the wheat extending nearly to the horizon.

(Enter Yago dressed as Nikey the Seer, wearing a green robe, dark glasses, and a rubber nose.)

YAGO

This brilliant disguise would fool even my Mum,
and though not a genius, she's certain not dumb.

(Puffs out his chest)
I'm Nikey the Seer, the wise man so sane,
wise enough to dupe Erik to harvest his grain
a full three weeks early while everything's green.
His farm will lose profits. I am *so* mean.

Ho! I do hear him, his heavy-trod feet,
coming quite near for this wise guy to meet.

(Enter Erik from stage left.)

ERIK

Excuse me, old man, are you Nikey the Seer?
A good man named Gobbo said you would pass near.

YAGO/NIKEY

He's Yago, good man. Yes, I'm Nikey all right.
But my seeing's retired.

ERIK

Yes, you have no sight.

YAGO/NIKEY

That sight does not matter, my third-sight's intact.
I quit because pay was not good. That's the fact.
Perhaps for a smoolie or four or fifteen,
I'll look around here and see what can be seen.

(Yago stands silently with hand extended, waiting.)

ERIK

Well . . . I do not know if it is worth the dough.
It's really quite silly. I really don't know.
I'm teensy bit worried . . . .

YAGO/NIKEY

. . . about your fine wheat.

ERIK

(Gaping in awe)
You know! You are wise! That was no small feat.
Will fifteen gold smoolies now get me some truths,
give me some good charms, and say me some sooths?

(Erik fishes fifteen gold smoolies from a pouch at his waist and hands them to Yago.)

YAGO/NIKEY

(Grinning)
I think these will do. Let us look at your field
and see what my wonderous third-sight will yield.

(Yago dances around waving his arms.)

YAGO/NIKEY

(Nodding wisely)
Just as I thought. Your wheat has the blight.
You and your family will not live the night
if you don't kill the warriors possessing your grain.
This may not be easy and may mean much pain.

ERIK

(Punches one mighty fist into the air)
Calloo and Callay! I am off for the war!
I'll show all those nasty grain warriors what for!
All of the gods will now see what I do!
DWICK, BRING MY ARMOR AND MY SWORDS, TOO!

YAGO/NIKEY

(Grabs Erik's arm to get his attention)
If you survive this, a god comes next eve
in disguise to reward you. You'd better believe.
Spengle, the wise God of Unbalanced Fights,
with red hair like mine, and bright blue-green tights
will offer you wisdom. You had better heed,
or else a brand new head as replacement you'll need.

ERIK

(Impatiently)
Yes, yes. Go away. I heard . . . now I'm bored.
DWICKY, YOU SLOWPOKE! BRING ME MY SWORD!

(Erik turns toward stage left, turning his back on Yago. Yago quickly runs behind the barn unseen. Enter Dwick (and puppet), from stage left, carrying Erik's sword, helmet, and body armor.)

DWICK

(Looking around fearfully)
What is it, "the Mighty"? Foul hordes of nast freaks?
Perhaps situation is not for the meek.
Here is your sword. I'll go back inside.
But, wait . . . I see no one afar or a-wide.

ERIK

(Gestures behind himself)
This kindly old man here has warned me a-right.
The wheat will attack us before end of night!

DWICK

Old man? Killer wheat? I see none of that here.

(Aside, to puppet.)
All of a sudden this seems very queer.

(Erik, surprised, turns around and sees that Nikey the Seer is not there.)

ERIK

Really, he *was* here . . . a blind, seeing man!
He told me the wheat has attack as their plan!

(Pause, then smiling grimly)
It must have been gods setting up hero's task.
"What will I do with the wheat?" you should ask!

DWICK

What will you do with the wheat? It's just grain.

ERIK

(Emphatically)
It's wheat-headed warriors all destined for pain
at the edge of my sword and the point of my knife!

(Points at dar moft Dwick)
I do this, good Dwicky, to save all our lifes.

(Erik proceeds to put on his armor and sword belt and turns to the wheat field at stage right.)

DWICK

(Aside, to puppet.)
Is whole Mighty family gone wrong in the head?
If he keeps up this madness, I'll be worse than dead.
At any time soon the book-maker will come
to talk with brave Erik. My head's going numb.

He'll never print stories of all our fine deeds,
(fulfilling well all my desires & greed)
if Erik is slashing at crops with his blade.
Blast! And I thought that I had it well made.

ERIK

(Angrily, walking toward the wheat)
Dwick, watch my back! They may creep up behind.

DWICK

(Aside, to puppet.)
This wheat does not look like the creeping up kind.

ERIK

Stop muttering, Dwicky, when danger's around.
If something goes wrong, we're all Underwhere bound.

DWICK

(Looking around frantically)
Mayhaps you can wait for a day, maybe three,
To see if the wheat-stalks in terror do flee.
Would you not rather tell stories of wars
And heroing deeds . . . and then tell some more?

(Acting casually)
Perhaps to a stranger . . . or book-making type.
Coincidentally, time is now ripe
for Sarcasto the Published to come by near here.
I'm sure all your stories would quite catch his ear.

ERIK

(Poking curiously with his sword at the nearest wheat stalk)
No, Dwick. I'm too busy saving our lives.
Cover my back if you want to survive.
Can't you see evil beset in the eyes
of those horricious, grainy, and stalky wheat-guys?

(Enter Yago, Crontobasticon, and Algimemmitoes from the barn. They remain near the barn, with Yago whispering to the cows animatedly.)

ERIK

(Striding into the wheat, sword poised to swing)
I'm off to the fray! Wish me luck in my stand!
If you have some time, you could lend me a hand.
I'm only outnumbered 12 million to one,
and not only out here for having some fun.

DWICK

(Waves one hand, dismissively)
No, you're the farmer . . . and I have sore wrists.
Besides, I'm a dar moft. You think I'd enlist?

(Aside to puppet.)
I won't go near him when he swings his sharp sword.
He's been carried away in the past as he's warred.
Sometimes in battle he thinks that he be
the swordsman Max Walrus, the hero of Glee.

ERIK

While you mutter, Dwicky, I'll save our old hides!
These wheats will be wishing to change fighting sides!

(Erik moves into the wheat and exits stage right. Slashing and fighting sounds can be heard.)

ERIK

HAVE AT YOU, NAST WHEATIES!! TASTE OF MY BLADE!!
AND YOU, AND YOU . . . HA! NOW YOU'RE AFRAID!!

(Yago moves toward Dwick. The cows remain near the barn, eyeballing the proceedings suspiciously.)

YAGO

(Innocently)
Nice day for a harvest, but isn't wheat green?
And harvest by swordplay I never have seen.

DWICK

(Shrugs)
It's tragic, strange Noggin.

YAGO

That's Yago. Go on.

DWICK

Erik's attacking the wheat. His mind's gone.
He thinks that the wheat wants to grain us to death
Unless he now fights them until dying breath.

YAGO

(Nods)
Yes, that is tragic . . .

DWICK

(Raises one green hand to interrupt)
That's not tragic part.
The tragedy has now but barely to start.
I'm trying to publish our traveling tales
and hope to make lots of big smoolies in sales.
So, I called on Sarcasto, a publishing type
to talk to brave Erik. The time is now ripe
for him to arrive.

(Dwick points down the road off stage right.)
There . . . that's him now!

YAGO

Excuse me, I have to go talk to the cows.

(Yago walks to the barn toward the cows.)

DWICK

(Angrily, aside to puppet)
I don't even like him. Why did I speak
of my terrible troubles to such a strange freak?

(Erik is still attacking the wheat field. Noise from the offstage battle becomes louder. Pieces of wheat stalks occasionally fly onto the stage.)

YAGO

Listen my spy-cows, you see that man there?
(Gestures down the road off stage)

CRONTOBASTICON

(Looks off stage at the approaching Sarcasto)
The man-thing with thinningish, balding, grey hair?

YAGO

The Erik-imposter is friends with that man,
and they're meeting together to plan some bad plans
to ruin your farm. They will start with the wheat,
but soon they will mow all the grass that you eat!

ALGIMEMMITOES

Ooh, that makes me mad. I like the tall blades.
He's going to get hoofy kick, I'm afraid!

CRONTOBASTICON

(Raising her hoofs as if to fight)
Let's get yon man, Algi! I'll steal his pants!
You grab some rocks, and we'll make him dance

(Algimemmitoes and Crontobasticon exit stage right. Erik continues to fight the wheat bravely.)

ERIK

(Voice heard from off-stage, occasional flurries of wheat stalk flying onto the stage)
BACK, YOU WHEAT NASTIES! YOUR LIVES ARE NOW THROUGH!
FOR I AM THE WALRUS! KOO KOO KA-CHOO!

(Enter Tenassity, Facsimili, and Facsimily from stage left. They stand behind Dwick, watching Erik in amazement. Dwick does not see them standing behind him.)

TENASSITY

Dwick, what's he doing? He harvests the wheat
And now grinds all plants beneath boot-shod feet!

And what are the cows doing with that man's pants?
Now they throw rocks at his feet so he'll dance!

DWICK

(Does not turn to talk to Tenassity, but turns his gaze in horror to the cows attacking Sarcasto.)

Oh no, no, no, no. Will the horror not end?
What do they do to Sarcasto, my friend?

FACSIMILI

(Amazed)
There they go, chasing him through the dead wheat!

FACSIMILY

It is right lucky that he has quick feet!
Oh, now father chases!

FACSIMILI

He tripped over cows!

TENASSITY

(Turns to Dwick)
Dwick, what has happened to cause all this row?

DWICK

(Still staring off stage)
Erik's gone crazy. He fights killer grain.

TENASSITY

(Turns to her daughters)
I hope Doctor Phyzzic can cure the insane.
Facsimili, Facsimily, go get the good Doc!
It will be only a four hour walk.

(Exit Facsimili and Facsimily, stage left. Enter Muckus from stage left. Enter Sarcasto (without his pants) from stage right, followed closely by Erik and the cows. Sarcasto stands near Dwick, Muckus, and Tenassity.)

ERIK

(Brandishing his sword threateningly toward Sarcasto)
Attack my fine watch cows will you, you foul cad!
Rustling my cattle does make me quite mad,
especially when I am so busy at war!
I am Max Walrus . . . AND YOU ARE NO MORE!

(Erik lunges toward Sarcasto, but Sarcasto grabs Muckus as a shield in front of him.)

SARCASTO

(Frightened)
No! You stand back, or I'm biting your swine!

MUCKUS

(Struggling)
Oh, you foul fiend!

ERIK

On raw pork you'd dine?
You'll get trichinosis.

MUCKUS

(Defensively)
No, Erik. I'm clean,
And even the proper amounts fat and lean!

TENASSITY

(Angrily)
Leave him alone! I'll have no fighting here!
Something around here does seem mighty queer!

Cows, put your rocks away! Go to your stalls!
Your bovine behavior does all here appall!

(Erik stands with sword at the ready. Exit Algimemmitoes and Crontobasticon, angrily, into the barn.)

TENASSITY

(To Sarcasto)
And you . . . drop our piggy. It's your only chance
of leaving here safely, and wearing your pants.

(Sarcasto lets go of Muckus. Dwick starts sneaking away, quietly.)

TENASSITY

Hold you there, Dwick! When there's trouble involved
you're often the culprit. I want this resolved.

SARCASTO

Dwick? Is it you? Why'd you call me here now
to be beaten and tortured by old, stupid cows?
Now you'll never publish in this life or next,
Even in some little school-childling's text!

(Sarcastically)
If abuse is all over, I'd like to leave.
I've had a good time . . . but I like dry heaves.
Mayhaps you would all like to visit some day . . .
so I can have lawyer types put you away!!!!

(Sarcasto, breechless, exits stage right.)

DWICK

Wait, good Sarcasto! I am not to blame!
Please come again!

(Smiles lamely)

We're all glad you came!

(Aside to puppet)
There go my chances . . . , but wait, what if I
wear a disguise as a different guy?
But I still need Erik, that hero so big.
Perhaps I can get him to wear a dark wig.

(Exit Dwick, stage left, muttering to his puppet.)

ERIK

Why did you let rustler go? He's no friend!

TENASSITY

Erik, this madness must here and now end!
Leave the wheat be, and come now to bed.
The doctor comes soon, and he's good at sick heads.

ERIK

(Waving his sword crazily, while others stand back nervously)
I know you need help, Ten. I'm glad you realize,
But I've still much to do while light stays in the skies.
We'll all be Underwhere bound if I fail.
You work on your brain while I kick grainy tail!

(Exit Erik, stage right, back to the Wheat War.)

ERIK

HO! NASTY WHEATIES, YOUR TIME IS AT END!
THE GRAIN FROM YOUR GREEN STALKS I'LL EASILY REND.
I'M WARRIOR KLAUS STALVART OF VEGOTNOFEERS!
CRINGE, YOU GRAIN NASTIES! BE OF BAD CHEER!

(Tenassity, now alone, watches the offstage battle sadly. Yago stands by the barn, laughing. Enter the Chorus from stage left. The lights slowly dim toward night as the Chorus sings.)

CHORUS

So Erik the Mighty does fall for foul play
and hack-saws at wheat stalks 'til end of the day.
Hi wife watches sadly while he fights a war
with unripened grain, wishing "no more".
He battled and sliced a full twelve hours long,
Slashing with blade, his fast arm big and strong,
Until every stalk of the enemy fell.
Now old man Erik does not look too well.

(Exit Chorus, stage left. Enter Facsimili, Facsimily, and Doctor Phyzzic from stage left. Enter Erik, smiling and staggering from stage right.)

ERIK

I did it, my Tenny. We're all safe tonight.
Those nasty wheat warriors can give us no fright.

(Looks at Facsimili and Facsimily, puzzled.)
I am so tired from all of this trouble
for now I believe that I am seeing double.

(Erik passes out, collapsing in a heap on the ground.)

Act II, Scene II

In which Doctor Phyzzic speaks of enemas, Erik speaks of enemies, Yago warns of copies, and Erik attacks his kitchen and family.

Eveningtime. Inside the kitchen of Erik the Mighty: To stage left and right, there are doors. At center stage there is a large cooking hearth, reddishly aglow from the fire, and two heavy wooden chairs. Kitchen utensils (pots, pans, knives, wooden spoons, etc . . .) hand from hooks on the wall. A large table stands to the rear left, next to the refrigerator and tall shelves with cans and a toaster. A large window is on the rear wall at the right. The Chorus stands at center stage, illuminated by a single spotlight while the rest of the stage is dim.

CHORUS

Erik the Mighty is worn from his fight
Which lasted all day and part into the night.
He but needs rest, although some think him mad.
They don't know the fault lies in Yago, the cad.

(Exit Chorus, stage right as the lights arise. Enter Facsimil and, Facsimily from stage left. They carry pillows and a pile of blankets and begin preparing the chair by the warm hearth for their father.)

FACSIMILI

Oh, sister. What can be done about this?
Father's gone mad. What can we do, Sis?

FACSIMILY

Maybe he's not mad, but just needs some rest.
He's been gone so long that he's not at his best.

What worries me most is our wheat is all dead.
And green wheat's not good in the making of bread.
When father realizes what he has just done,
he'll be upset. We'll earn smoolies not one.

FACSIMILI

Wait, I was talking to Yabo out there.
Maybe there is a solution somewhere . . .
He says we can easily make green-wheat wine,
Using slain wheat and these here bulbs so fine!

(Facsimili gestures to six large bulbs of garlic, which she has hidden in her apron.)

FACSIMILI

He calls them zucchinis, whatever they be.
They're used in "speed-wining" quite often, says he.
It takes only days to ferment the green wheat.
So, saving lost profits will be no large feat!
And wine's worth much smooly at marketing place.
We can recover from Daddy Headcase.

FACSIMILY

Yes, but we mustn't tell anyone this.
We'll brew it in dark basement, secretly, Sis.

FACSIMILI

Hush, they do come now. They're bearing our dad.
Let's leave to discuss the ideas we've had.

(Exit Facsimili and Facsimily, stage right. Enter Doctor Phyzzic and Tenassity, half carrying, half dragging Erik into the kitchen from stage left. They sit him carefully in the blanketed chair by the hearth.)

TENASSITY

Doctor, oh Doctor. Please can you help him?
He's losing his mind. His brain has gone dim.

DR. PHYZZIC

(Musing)
What causes his problem I cannot be sure,
but I'm fairly certain that I have a cure.
In all of my studies, I've noted a trend.
The brain's oft affected by . . . the other end.
An enema is the solution preferred
for many afflictions. He will be cured.

I once met a man who had warts on his head
so painful that he wished that he'd been born dead.
After one enema, warts went away!!!
He is quite happy . . . to this very day.
Another time, I met a man who was ill.
No cure could be found inside any small pill.
After two enemas he became well!
Many's the story that I have to tell.

The enema cleanses the soul from inside,
flushing foul spirits afar and awide,
and refreshing one well. I have three a day.
They do work miracles. You'll see the way
that Erik's mad brain will revive and be free!
Enemas! Enemas! They are the key!

TENASSITY

Well, go on, Doctor. Don't waste any time.
Let's do it while he is still sleeping sublime.

(Erik awakens and sits up slowly in his chair.)

ERIK

Enemies, enemies? Where are they, Ten?
I'll slice them, I'll dice them . . . and all of their ken!

TENASSITY

Not enemies . . . enemas. Doc says it will help
if we give you an enema. Sit still and don't yelp.

ERIK

Doc, how will my "enema" help Tenny's brain?

DR. PHYZZIC

She's not the one who attacked all the grain.

ERIK

I know. I did, Doctor. Of that I am proud.
What's that to do with her head in the clouds?

TENASSITY

Erik, sit quiet. It won't hurt a bit.
Maybe this enema can help out your wit.

ERIK

My fine sense of humor is needing no aid.
What is an enema . . . some juice of nightshade?

(Tenassity leans over and whispers into Erik's ear.)

ERIK

Oh, no. Not me! I won't sit for that!
What happened to leaches and blood-sucking bats?

DR. PHYZZIC

Medical knowledge does really progress
as the years pass. Now put on this dress.

(Dr. Phyzzic hands Erik a hospital gown.)

ERIK

Doc, are you mad? Do you know who I be?
I'm Erik the Mighty. You'd better flee!

(Erik raises his two mighty fists.)
Now, DOCTOR DUNG! You're a weird one, I think,
and your doctorly practices really do stink!

(Exit Dr. Phyzzic, running from Erik's menacing fists, stage right. Enter Yago from stage right, pausing at the doorway to chew a clove of garlic. He is nearly run down in the exit of the Doctor.)

YAGO

Excuse the intrusion. Please, might I speak
to Erik the Mighty? Or is he to weak
from his harvest last night? Could we speak alone?
I won't stay long at the sicko's hearthstone.

ERIK

Leave, Ten. Don't worry. There must be some means
to cure your brain-fever . . . that's little more clean.

I'll talk to Goober and then get more rest.
The morrow may bring me some more godly tests.

TENASSITY

(Reluctantly)
Rest well, my husband, and later we'll talk
of strangely obsessions. We'll take a nice walk.

(Tenassity exits stage left.)

ERIK

What brings you, Booger? Impressed by my might?

YAGO

(Aside, muttering)
The might of your brain becomes ever so slight.

ERIK

What?

YAGO

I said, "You're ever so mighty with blade."

ERIK

That's what I thought you said. Don't be afraid.
I only fight evilly, foul, nasty sorts.
Pull up yon chair and bring butt into port.
What brings you by, Doobie? Spit it out, boy.

YAGO

Well, Mighty Erik, it brings me no joy
to tell you this news. There is trouble at hand.
You know that dark evil that was in your land?
It's now in your homestead, right here in this room.
If you don't kill it, your family is doomed.

ERIK

I am not dweebish. Prove that this is true.
Many could talk of dark things 'til they're blue.

YAGO

I have no proof, Erik. Think of the wheat.
I foresaw that evil. It was no small feat!

(Shrugs and rises)
Well, my job is done. I have warned my good host.
I cannot be blamed for I tried my utmost.

(Yago bows to Erik and exits stage left.)

ERIK

Maybe he's right. He spoke true about grain.
Besides, in a lie what would he have to gain?

I'll call him back. He cannot be far.
I'll give him some ade and a smelly cigar.

(Enter Yago from stage left, dressed as Spengle, the God of Unbalanced Fights, wearing bright blue-green tights, a mask over his eyes, and a pointy rubber nose.)

ERIK

Who are *you*?

YAGO/SPENGLE

I am God Spengle, the Great,
and I have an important job that can't wait
for you to do well. Down on your knees!
Your lack of respect here does not muchly please.

ERIK

(He kneels)
Forgive me, oh Spengle. It's all new to me.
I never learned etiquette. Do you want some tea?

YAGO/SPENGLE

Forget it. I have troubled matters to speak,
things not for the wimpy and not for the weak.
Demons possess all your fine kitchen stuff,
your pots and your pans, and if that's not enough,
they even now plan to possess your family.
Some of this already happens to be.

First they make copies of family and friends,
then they replace them! This horror won't end
until you destroy all the things foul-possessed.
Take deadly measures! This isn't a test!

And beware, trust of no one, not even your wife,
if you still wish to save all of your lives.
So, don't turn your back on the pots and the pans,
oven mitts, skewers, steak knives, food-filled cans,
oven, refrigerator, or lovely daughter.

The only sure cure is death . . . blood . . . and slaughter.

(Exit Yago/Spengle, stage left.)

ERIK

Wait, Spengle, wait! Oh, no. Somebody comes!
I must keep this secret 'til I conjure some
plan of attacking. No one can I trust.
I'm all alone, but succeed well, I must!
I'll sit me down and pretend that I nap
to overhear clues for this evil to trap!

(Erik feigns sleep, as Tenassity, Facsimili, and Facsimily enter from stage right.)

TENASSITY

Quietly now, for your father does sleep.
We must prepare dinner without making peeps.
Facsimili, tell Dwick that he must bring in wood,
while Facsimily and I do prepare the food-goods.

(Exit Facsimili, stage right. Erik sits up and looks around curiously, sees only Tenassity and Facsimily (who are at the table with their backs toward him), and resumes his false napping.)

TENASSITY

My girl, get the pot from the wall over there.
It's up rather high, so you may need a chair.

(Facsimily moves the chair next to Erik over to the wall. As she reaches for the pot, she stumbles, shrieks, and drops the pot onto the floor. Erik leaps to the rescue, kicking and stomping the pot with his feet.)

ERIK:

Aha! I got one! You'll regret the day
that you tussled with Erik in frenze-bloody fray!
Take that! Taste my boots! You foul, metal fiend.
I'll be the last sight that you've ever seen!

(Tenassity and Facsimily stand amazed, watching. Erik calmly returns to his chair.)

ERIK

Sorry, dear Tenny. I . . . um . . . hate when pans fall.
Stomping them . . . uh . . . brings good luck to us all.

TENASSITY

(Puzzled, she picks up the dented, flattened pan)
Good. Now you rest. You've had quite a long day.

ERIK

All right, Tenny. I won't get in your way.

(Aside)
I must destroy all of the pots and the pans
before the foul evil can finish its plans
to hurt my fine family. It's lucky I'm here.
I can end problems. Of that I've no fear!

(Erik wraps himself tighter in his blankets and sits by the hearth. The suspicious faces of Crontobasticon and Algimemmitoes appear at the window. Yago also appears, feeding them garlic cloves.)

FACSIMILY

Mother, shall I chop some spuds for the meal?

TENASSITY

Bring them here and I will help you to peel
. . . and all of the other fresh veggies. We will
slice them and dice them to put in the swill.

(Facsimily brings a large basket full of potatoes and vegetables to her mother. They talk quietly as they prepare the meal, with their backs toward Erik.)

(Erik looks carefully and suspiciously at the various cooking utensils in the kitchen as he sits by the hearth.)

FACSIMILY

Mother, will father get well in near days?
I hope that this is just a passing bad phase.

TENASSITY

Let's hope that it's so, dear Facsimily.
We cannot afford things to stay as they be.
We need many smoolies to keep out the cold,
and loss of our wheat may be dire strangle-hold.

(Erik reaches quietly over to the wall and removes a cleaver from the knife rack. He looks it over carefully, then he begins strangling the handle. Not quite satisfied, he breaks the cleaver over his knee. Happily, he conceals the dead body in one of his blankets and sets it on the floor.)

(The cows look in horror from the window. Yago gestures for them to wait and be watchful.)

FACSIMILY

Is there no way we can make up the loss?
Perhaps our green wheat could bring lesser the cost.

(Erik grabs a large wooden spoon from the wall and breaks it with a crisp "SNAP". He conceals the body in the blanket and feigns sleep just as Tenassity and Facsimily turn in response to the wood-snapping noise. Crontobasticon's angry face glares from the window.)

TENASSITY

I'm worried. Your father just seemed to have "snapped".
Now he lays quietly taking a nap,
but what will he do when the morrow arrives?

FACSIMILY

Certainly you're not afraid for our lives?

TENASSITY

Oh, no! Not that. I fear for our farm.
I don't know what other things he will harm.

(Enter Facsimili from stage right, walking unsteadily. She carries a glass of green-wheat wine in her left had and a string of garlic bulbs in her right. She beckons to her sister. Erik still feigns sleep.)

(Facsimili walks over to her and they whisper together at the front of stage left.)

FACSIMILI

(Gently swaying)
Sister, I bring you the first of our wine.
I've sampled it some, and I think it is fine.

(She waves the garlic bulbs drunkenly.)
This zuchini stuff can really do tricks.
Try it. You'll like it. Our problems are fixed

FACSIMILY

Go back and make more. We need much, much more
if we're to succeed and our homestead restore.

(Facsimili hands the glass to her sister and walks toward stage right to exit. She pauses behind her father's chair, looking at him with concern.)

FACSIMILI:

Facsimily?

FACSIMILY

Yes, Facs?

FACSIMILI

Is father all right?

FACSIMILY

I know not. He's been quiet all of the night.

(Erik opens his eyes in surprise at hearing his daughter's voice in two places. As he turns to look behind him, Facsimili drops her garlic bulbs and bends over to retrieve them. He does not see her behind the chair. Facsimily takes her fathers arm, encouraging him to relax in his chair to rest. Erik shrugs and returns to his false napping.)

(Facsimili weavingly exits stage right. Facsimily returns to her mother's side to slice vegetables.)

(Erik stands and tip-toes around the kitchen, looking for suspicious objects. He quickly grabs pot after pan after pot, strangling them each in turn and concealing them in the blankets by the chair. He grabs

the toaster, bear-hugs it crushingly and tosses it in with the other dead bodies. The cows gaze in amazement from the window.)

(The cows disappear from the window and enter from stage right, wobbling and weaving in garlic stupor. They attack Erik, trying to wrestle him to the floor. Tenassity and Facsimily turn around at the sudden noise of the scuffle.)

ERIK

(Wrestling with two cows)
Ho! Stop it cow-girls. Have you gone mad?

TENASSITY

(Angrily, turns to confront the cows)
Cronto and Algi! You're acting quite bad!

(Crontobasticon and Algimemmitoes stop assaulting Erik and stand quietly, weaving, gasping for breath.)

CRONTOBASTICON

We saw this stranger assaulting yer pots!

TENASSITY

He's not a stranger, you two bovine sots!
He's Erik the Mighty, my husband, my man.
Go to the barn or your two hides I'll tan.
You act like you've grazed in the mushrooms once more.
You weave and you bob as if on moving floor!
Go! I said go! My Erik needs rest.

(Aside)
Lately it seems that the world is possessed!

(Exit cows, muttering and weaving, stage right. Tenassity guides Erik tenderly back to his chair.)

TENASSITY

(Holds Erik's arm as he sits)
Are you all right Erik? Please, sit at ease.

ERIK

Perhaps they just have that new "mad cow" disease.

(Erik yawns a big, fake yawn and closes his eyes once again. Facsimily and Tenassity return to the veggie chopping.)

TENASSITY

(To Facsimily)
Dear, get the cleaver from off of the wall.

(Facsimily walks past the napping Erik to get the cleaver, pauses, and looks all around.)

FACSIMILY

Mother, those cow-girls are so full of gall!
They've taken the knives and pots! We have none!

TENASSITY

(Angrily)
They will regret all of this when I'm done!

(Enter Facsimili, weaving, from stage right. She carries a large jug of green-wheat garlic wine and weaves unsteadily.)

FACSIMILI

What's going on? I saw cows leaving mad.

TENASSITY

I don't know Facs, but the cows have been bad.

(Erik opens his eyes and gazes in horror at his two identical daughters. He leaps to his feet. Yago, once again is peering from the window.)

ERIK

DWICK, BRING MY SWORD! BRING IT HERE QUICK!

TENASSITY

(Alarmed)
You don't need your sword. The cows are just sick.

ERIK

(Pauses)
I only wish to . . . um . . . clean my sword well.
It's covered with plant blood from wheat that I felled.

(Enter Dwick, running, from stage left. He is wearing a dark wig and carrying a blond wig, Erik's sword, and armor. Erik is facing stage right (and the weaving Facsimili) as Dwick hands him his sword from behind.)

DWICK

What is the matter, brave Erik? More grain?

ERIK

(Points angrily at his Facsimili)
NO! A FALSE DAUGHTER. IS IT NOT PLAIN?

(Erik chases after the garlicked Facsimili, who shrieks and runs over to her sister and mother. Erik suddenly notices Dwick in his dark wig.)

ERIK

They got to you, too, gentle Dwicky. Too bad
but I must kill you both. It makes me quite sad.

DWICK

No, It's me, Dwick! This is just a dark wig
to fool that Sarcasto. Here's one more . . . big
to fit your large head. Please, Erik. Cease!
I'd never make you wear any hairpiece.

(Erik chases both Facsimili and Dwick around the room.)

TENASSITY

(Moves in front of Erik)
Stop it, please! Erik! Please drop your blade!
This is a bad, bad mistake that you've made!

ERIK

Tell them to stop. I can't kill them when
they keep moving 'bout like a couple of hens.

(Erik pauses with his back to Tenassity. She grabs a large can of Spam from the near shelf and hits him on the head. Erik collapses to the floor.)

TENASSITY

(Weeping)
Bring the cows out and lock *him* in the barn.
I'll tie him up with some strongly weaved yarn.

(Enter Yago from stage right, carrying heavy rope.)

YAGO

Allow me to help. The hurt is too great
for you to tie up your long life's love-mate.

TENASSITY

Thank you, good Bloggo. You are so kind.
I'm sorry your visit did craziness find.

(Yago ties Erik's hands and feet and drags him across the kitchen floor toward stage right while Tenassity weeps and his daughters gaze in shock.)

YAGO

(Pausing in his dragging efforts)
I'll try to reason with this crazy guy.
Perhaps you should all sit, relax, . . . and wine try.

(Yago gestures to the jug in Facsimili's hand.)

YAGO

(Aside)
This is my chance now to make their lives messed.
I'll tell Erik that barn and farm tools are possessed
to make him attack. They'll never free him.
With garlicky wine I do make their minds dim.

I'm taking over. They'll do what I say.
In everything I will be having my way.

(Exit Yago, dragging Erik, stage right.)

DWICK

What a nice guy. And I thought he stank.

TENASSITY

I guess we all now know the one we should thank.

(Tenassity pours them each a glass of garlicky wine. They all drink.)

FACSIMILI

Yes. He is swell. I really like him.
To do kindly deeds he'd go out on a limb.

FACSIMILY

Let's let him stay. He seems so lonesome.

(Enter Crontobasticon, Algimemmitoes, and Muckus from stage right.)

MUCKUS

What's going on? I have just come
from the barn where that Zobbo has Erik all tied.
Can't you all stop him? Haven't you tried?

TENASSITY

Muckus, the truth is quite hard to tell you.
Erik's gone mad. He's crazed through and through.

ALGIMEMMITOES

Globo does help him. He's calming him down.
The two of them whisper and make little sound.

DWICK

If anyone can, good old Blobbo can save
Erik from madly mind's rantings and raves.

(Tenassity pours the pig and cows some wine and refills the glases of the others. Dwick holds his glass aloft in puppeted hand.)

DWICK

(Weeping)
A toast! To good Poohbah. He's one of a kind.
The bestest of friends that any could find!

(They all drink somberly. Enter Yago, feigning sadness, from stage left.)

YAGO

Bad news, my friends. He would not heed
my friendly reason. And now he is freed
but still locked in the barn. He has the crazed thought
that a battle with barn really needs to be fought.
He thinks that an evil possesses his tools.

I'm sorry, my friends. He is a crazed fool.

TENASSITY

Oh, no. My poor Erik. He's had a bad life.
He's had too much traveling and too much strife.
Bobo, what is there that we can now do?

YAGO

Your options are clearly much less than a few.
He must not leave barn for the rest of his days.
It's for the best. He's much, much too crazed.

(Tenassity sits heavily upon one of the chairs by the hearth. Facsimili, Muckus, and Facsimily weep drunkenly. Dwick stares in silence. The cows and Yago drink heavily.)

(Enter the Chorus from stage left.)

CHORUS

They drink for a while until each fall asleep.
excepting for Yago, that foul, nasty creep.
Is he succeeding in horrible plot?
Certainly we hope that *you* hope he is not.
We wish Yago ending in some icky way,
shaved, painted purple, and put on display,
then put on a bus to a place where men hate
foul, purple men with a shaved, balding pate.

YAGO

Out, out foul Chorus! I have won this one.
I certainly had a whole bushel of fun!

(Exit Chorus sadly, stage left. Yago dances around the room, laughing foully and jumping over the drunken bodies of the Mighty family.)

YAGO

Now *I'm* in control. I've revenged Spunky true,
but there's still much more that I have to do.
Tomorrow I ruin the rest of their lives.
Then I kill Erik. For all this I strive.

Erik Miteus

LAST ACT

Last Act, Last Scene

In which Yago rules the roost and tries to eat Muckus, and Erik escapes to do battle.

Morningtime. Inside the farmhouse of Erik the Mighty: In the center of the room is an enormous fireplace and hearth with a large chair. Yago, the cows, the pig, Tenasity, Facsimili, Facsimily, and Dwick sit, at the large kitchen table together on one side of the room. All but Yago are smiling broad, dazed smiles.

(Enter Chorus, stage left.)

CHORUS

It's morningtime inside of Yago's fine farm.
Erik's in barn where he can't do more harm.
Yago has duped and he's doped all the rest.
But he's not done yet. Don't relax lest
he convince you, too. He has clever brain.
He has nothing to lose and revenging to gain.

(Exit Chorus, stage left.)

YAGO

Good morning, my friends. I trust you slept well?
I hope that you found that your breakfast was swell.

TENASSITY

Thank you, fine Rozzo. You are too kind.
This morning it was quite surprising to find
the breakfast all made and awaiting for us.
And you used zucchini and made such a fuss.

FACSIMILI

(Smiling)
After the breakfast, I don't feel so sad,
yet when I awoke I felt awesomely bad.

YAGO

Oft times good breakfasts will revive your brain,
and help you forget all your troubles and pains.

(Aside)
Especially when garlic's used at low dose.
Garlic can cure the acutely morose.

(They all nod and smile happily.)

DWICK

You said you had something important to say?

(Aside, to puppet)
I hope that he now is deciding to stay!

YAGO

(Feigning reluctance)
I've thought about what you all asked me this morn.
Frankly, good folks, I am really quite torn,
but I have decided to stay with you here.
I'll be a fine leader. So have you no fear.

MUCKUS

I prefer Erik. He's kindly and good.

TENASSITY

(Alarmed)
Muckus, your manners! I think that you should
say "sorry" to Jimbo. Right now, little swine.
You shouldn't insult a good man who's so fine.

CRONTOBASTICON

(Aside to Algimemmitoes)
I really am glad that fine Stinko don't leave.

ALGIMEMMITOES

(Aside to Crontobasticon)
I'd really miss wheat-wine. If gone I would grieve.

FACSIMILI

What now will happen without our wheat field?
Do you think our wine can replace our wheat yield?

YAGO

Perhaps not entire, but hear now what I've planned.
We'll plant zucchinis all over our lands.

TENASSITY

A wondrous idea! It's my favorite food.

DWICK

(Aside, to puppet)
Yoblo is frabjous. What a brained dude.

(Puppet shakes his head and covers his face.)

(Yago sighs. He stands up and looks at them sadly.)

YAGO

I said that this won't solve our problems entire.
We are still trapped in the Straits of the Dire.

TENASSITY

What can we do? You must have some plan,
being so smartish and brightly a man.

YAGO

I have a plan . . . but what rights have I.
I am not kin. I but merely dropped by.
Why should you listen to ought that I say.

TENASSITY

Whatever you say, Bobo. We'll go your way.

FACSIMILI

Yes, yes, good Dodo. We trust you complete.

DWICK

We'll do what you say. You now have leader's seat

(Yago sighs. He looks at them painedly and sits down.)

YAGO

These *are* hard decisions.

TENASSITY

Please, Frodo, speak.

YAGO

We must act quite strongly, and not wimpy-weak.

(Pause)
Dwick. You need a job now to bring in some pay.

TENASSITY

(To Dwick, patting him on the shoulder.)
Perhaps a store salesman, a quiet work day.

YAGO

No . . . job in the Basil Mines, mining for spice.
Cheer up, you work hard and you'll bring a good price.

(Dwick frowns sadly at his puppet, large nose quivering as he struggles not to weep.)

DWICK

If that's what must be, I will do it for you.

(Everyone stands to console Dwick and they turn to leave.)

YAGO

Wait! That's not all. We have more things to do.

(Turns to the daughters)
Facsimili, Facsimily, you both must be wed.
Not to each other . . . to old Squiff and Jed.

TENASSITY

(Shocked)
But they are town drunks! This I cannot allow!

YAGO

(Angrily)
You said you'd abide by my rules. Anyhow,
they have many smoolies, all hidden away.
I know they will give large, large dowries. Okay?

(Aside)
It's so fun to lie. Squiff and Jed *are* old bums.
But the best of my dastardly plan is to come.

FACSIMILI

Mother, we must. We all have agreed.

TENASSITY

(Quietly)
It hurts to wed roses to ugly old weeds.
But, you are correct. It won't be so bad.
Surprisingly, I do not feel very sad.

Is this all, Yado?

YAGO

Not quite, Lady Ten.
We must find good ways to feed you and your ken.
We have little meat, not enough to last long.
We must eat your pig.

MUCKUS

(Horrified)

No, no, no! This is wrong!

YAGO

Don't be so selfish. Should we all starve
to save you from being cooked up and then carved?

DWICK

(Patting Muckus on the head)
Yes. Don't be selfish. You have lots of meat.
There'll be enough for us all here to eat.

(Dwick's puppet shakes his head and covers his face.)

(Muckus runs to hide behind Tenassity.)

MUCKUS

Tenassity, help me. Would you eat pork?

TENASSITY

(Pauses, considering)
Not with a spoon, but I would with a fork.

(Muckus flees the room, stage right, screaming.)

FACSIMILY

Should we go catch him and eat him tonight?

YAGO

We'll catch him later. He'll get over fright.
We have some more things that must be discussed.

I need you to tell me if I have your trust.

TENASSITY

Yes! Yes, good Yanno. We need you around.
Since you came here, we've all happiness found.

YAGO

Good, for I have a proposal to make
which may sound so heartless, yet makes my heart ache.

It's about Erik. Do you wish that he
live rest of his life really crazed and unfree?

FACSIMILI

No! No, good Yobbo. His life's mockery.

YAGO

Then why not now finish his sad misery?

(All look dazed and shocked. Tenassity's head bows sadly.)

TENASSITY

Do you think that we must? Would it be too cruel
to keep him locked up? I love the old fool.

YAGO

Would Erik the Mighty now wish to be thought
by his whole family as a foolish sot?

TENASSITY

No, I guess not. But can't we just wait
to see if he 'scapes from his poor mental fate?

YAGO

But if he 'scapes from the barn now instead
whole Mighty family could wind up dead!!!

Here, have zucchini and let's think awhile.

(Aside)
They'll not escape from my Oontian guile.

(Yago hands out cloves of garlic to Mighty family, Dwick, and animals.)

DWICK

(Chewing garlic)
Thank you, fine Yondo. You're so generous.
I'm sorry I once called you malodorous.

YAGO

That's all right, Dwick. I've forgiven all.

(Aside)
Just wait . . . in the mines you will have a nice fall.

CRONTOBASTICON

(Weaving drunkenly)
Let's talk of Erik. I fear fer my hide.
He's an imposter who's lied, lied, and lied.
And he is crazy! Let's put him to death!

ALGIMEMMITOES

Yes, on this day we should all take his breath.

TENASSITY

(Crying)
No. He's my husband!

YAGO

Wait! I've solved it now!
I'll talk with him there & I'll soothe crazy brow,
and if he can calm down we'll keep him awhile.
But, if he fights or he seems to get riled
I'll have to defend myself, maybe take life.
I'm willing to risk myself for his fine wife.

(Aside)
Oh, this is brilliant, I'll rile him up well
and kill him in self-defense. This is so swell!
And none here will see. The garlic they ate
will any time now . . . incapacitate.

(Everyone, except Yago, becomes more garlic crazed and usteady on their feet. They all sway and smile laughingly.)

TENASSITY

(Falls at Yago's feet)
You are so kind, Yago. And quite brave, too!
Without you I don't know what we could do.

(Enter Muckus, followed by a double-sword flailing and muchly angered Erik.)

ERIK

You'd better learn, Ten. He won't be here, long!
At point of my sword he will sing his swan-song.

YAGO

See! I told you he's crazy. I'm his best friend,
yet he wants to give me some foul, bloody end!

TENASSITY

(Stands, weaving drunkenly)
Erik, please. Erik! You are not well!
We're on your side. Can you not tell?

ERIK

Muckus has told me all I need to know!
Bobbo has really put on quite a show.
I was a fool. I thought he told truth.
He planned evil ends when I thought he said sooth!

Take this sword, Dobby! We'll fight this like men.

(Erik throws one of his swords to Yago, who catches it by the hilt.)

Stand out of way, daughters. Back away, Ten.

(Suddenly the drunkenly weaving Facsimili, Facsimily, Tenassity, and the cows fall into a garlicked daze, collapsing to the floor. Dwick collapses unconscious onto one of the chaisr, puppeted hand upright and attentive. Muckus watches quietly with both front hooves to his mouth.)

YAGO

Don't worry about them. They're garlicked extreme.

ERIK

You're a fiend, Gobbo. I'll split your foul seam!

YAGO

(Slashing the air with his blade, masterfully)
You've met your match, Erik. I'm master of blade.
You cannot be thinking that I'll be afraid
and run away crazed like the others you've fought.

ERIK

Shut your mouth, Goober. Great speaker you're not.

(Yago lunges at Erik with slashing blade. Erik counters with his sword. They slash and parry, circling the room several times and leaping over the garlicked bodies of Erik's family and friends. It is a long and tiring fight with several circlings around the kitchen table. The puppet on the unconscious Dwick's hand continues to watch attentively.)

ERIK

I'm Erik the Mighty. Taste of my sword.

(Slash toward Yago's undefended side)

YAGO

(Spins around to parry Erik's blade, and he jumps back nimbly)
Just Erik the Mighty. I'm getting bored.
I thought you were Walrus, the warrior of Glee,
or are you Klaus Stalvart? Just who do you be?

ERIK

Erik the Mighty's enough match for you.
Doobie, your long, evil life is now through!

(Erik lunges at Yago, deswording him and forcing him to the floor at sword point, next to the sleeping Tenassity.)

ERIK

Say your prayers, Donny. It's all over now.

(Yago quickly pulls out a knife from his belt and holds it to Tenassity's throat.)

YAGO

Not so quick, Erik. I've made a strong vow
and I will kill any who get in my way.
Drop your sword, Erik . . . or wife I will flay.

(Erik throws his sword to the floor, near Dwick's feet. Yago picks up his own sword and stands. He advances on Erik.)

(Suddenly, Muckus runs up to Yago and kicks him in the shins with his cloved hooves. Yago glares at Muckus.)

MUCKUS

Back, you foul brute. Leave Erik alone.

YAGO

(Looking hungrily at Muckus)
I wonder how quickly this pig will de-bone?

(Yago hurls the piggy across the room. He continues advancing upon Erik. Dwick's puppet begins tapping Dwick sharply upon the head. Dwick stirs.)

YAGO

Erik the Mighty. You killed my best friend
when you sank my fine kree, a foul and wet end.
Your nast battle-kree with it's flag, icky blue,
killed my poor Spunky.

(Advances slowly on Erik.)

So I will kill you.

(Dwick's puppet continues tapping Dwick's head until Dwick awakes and dazedly looks at what is happening. The puppet gestures to the sword at Dwick's feet.)

YAGO

(Raises his sword overhead)
Spunky, my hamster was such a fine soul,
muchly much nicer than former pet vole.
He sang and he danced well. He really loved me.
You came and killed him with your blue kree.

(As Yago is about to deal Erik a mortal blow with his sword, Dwick, with puppeted hand, picks up the sword from the floor and throws it to Erik.

(Erik pierces Yago with his sword before Yago can swing his blade down. Yago drops his sword and steps back, hands holding his wound.)

YAGO

This really sucks. So much for revenge.
The foul rodent-killer has met my challenge.

I'm so sorry, Spunky. He's gotten away,
and in the process he managed to slay
a fine human being. Yes, I'm quite dead,
though Erik the Mighty should be dead instead.

ERIK

I seem to recall that you mentioned blue flag?

YAGO

Don't torment me, Erik. I'm starting to sag.

ERIK

Did you say blue?

YAGO

Yes, I did. Let me be.

ERIK

Erik the Blue was your man. It's not me
you were after. I never had sank
a ship in that war. I must be quite frank.

YAGO

(Staring at Crontobasticon' sleeping form)
Spunky, oh Spunky. I see you now.
You're dancing so nice on the head of that cow.

ERIK

Did you not hear me? I said you were wrong.

YAGO

(Looking to the heavens)
Spunky, oh Spunky. I love your fine song.
The thickets are chirping. The egg stands alone.
I hear something ringing. Will you get the phone?

ERIK

Besides, it was war. I'm sure Erik the Blue
had quite a good reason for sinking your crew.

(Yago falls to his knees.)

YAGO

(Gasping)
It's getting black . . . well, maybe dark gray.
I'm glad I killed Erik. I made him pay.

(Yago collapses and dies. Erik stands over him quietly as Tenassity, Facsimili, Facsimily, the cows, and Muckus begin to awaken.)

DWICK

(Jumps to his feet unsteadily)
Tenassity! Erik was sane after all.
Yago was crazed, and he plotted our fall
for some silly rodent. Erik slew him
. . .and we all thought Erik's brain had gone dim.

(Dwick's puppet nods wisely.)

TENASSITY

(Runs to Erik's arms)
Erik, we're sorry. We didn't know.
Girls, go get father some water. Now, go!

(Facsimili and Facsimily exit stage left.)

ALGIMEMMITOES

We're sorry, Erik. We're just stupid cows,
and he fed us garlic instead of our chow.

ERIK

(Embraces Tenassity)
This fiend was brilliant. He even fooled me.
I was convinced so that strange things I'd see.

(Enter Erik the Mighty's son, Harry, from stage left, wearing a long, black wig and a bright blue dress. He looks remarkably like his sisters.)

HARRY

Father? I'm Harry!

ERIK

(Looks curiously at the new arrival.)

You *do* need a shave.

(Enter Facsimily and Facsimili from stage left with a large glass of water. They stand next to Harry. Erik's eyes open wide and he reaches for his sword.)

ERIK

(Shocked)
Oh no! It happens again. I will save
us all from this evil! DEATH MUST BE DONE!

(Erik chases Harry around the room.)

TENASSITY

(Jumps between Erik and Harry)
No! Oh no, Erik! That's Harry, your son.
Women sell grain better at market place,
so Harry wears dresses and paints up his face.

ERIK

(Stops his chase and lowers his sword.)
Sorry, son. I thought you were demon-spawn.

HARRY

(Frowning)
Gee, I thought I looked pretty good with dress on.
What happened here? And who's the dead guy?

TENASSITY

I'll tell you later the hows and the why.
Come here the rest of you, Dwick, girls, cows, pig!
Erik can rest while the rest of us dig.

(Exit Tenassity, Facsimili, Facsimily, Harry, Dwick, Muckus, and the cows, dragging Yago's body stage right. Erik sits down in a large chair by the hearth.)

ERIK

(Musing)
I guess I'm a hero, now. It's about time.
Just when I thought to start taking up mime.

(Enter Moose, the god of all gods in Olmpoo, in a cloud of dust. He is tall and strong, with a long grey beard, and he wears glittery, godly robes.)

MOOSE

Erik, I'm Moose. You are quite a brave guy.
I'll reward you with what smoolies can't buy.
I'll make you a god and you'll sit by my side.

ERIK

(Examines Moose doubtfully)

You couldn't make rocks. I think your brain's fried.
You're just some bad garlic that I must have ate.
Why don't you leave now. You mustn't be late.

(Aside)
Imagine him thinking that I am a fool.
Moose, I think not. But his outfit is cool.

MOOSE

(Angrily)
YOU DARE TO MOCK ME? A ROCK YOU WILL BE!
Quickly your errors in thoughts you will see!

(Moose, with a wave of his godly arms, turns Erik into a large rock. Erik the Mighty Rock sits quietly in his chair as Moose disappears in a cloud of dust.)

ERIK

Hey! This is great. That WAS Moose that was here!
Tenassity, Dwick! Hurry! Come you both near!

(Enter Dwick, Facsimili, Facsimily, Tenassity, Muckus, and the cows from stage right.)

TENASSITY

Erik? Where *are* you? I see just a rock!

ERIK

(Rockishly)
The rock is now me! Don't just stand there and gawk.

TENASSITY

(Weeping)
Erik, it's awful.

ERIK

No, you have it wrong.
I'll live forever in folklore and song.
Erik the Mighty will be famous now!

DWICK

But you're a rock!

ERIK

(Proudly)
It's still honorful how
Moose came to me and then turned me to stone.
Moose came to me! Me, Erik! Alone!

DWICK

(Sputtering)
But you're a rock!

ERIK

Does it matter that much?
What of the legend of Dweezil and Dutch?
They turned into Spam for no reason at all.
Or how about King Muffler's ego-ly fall!
He turned into salt. At least I am stone.
And I have you all, so I'll not be alone!

FACSIMILY

(Tearfully)
Yes, we are here for you. We will not leave.
And if you're happy we'll not even grieve.

DWICK

(Now excited)
We could make profits by showing you 'round.
Imagine, a rock that makes talking sounds!
We'll make up for lost grain, and earn smoolies too!

ALGIMEMMITOES

(Smiling cowishly)
With the right saddle, we can carry you!

(Crontobasticon nods eagerly.)

(Enter Chorus from stage left.)

CHORUS

So all has well ended, though Erik is stone.
Erik's made up for his lost roams alone.

He got his chance as a heroing type.
Dwick will now start up the media hype
and sell Erik's story (all told quite true)
to make TV series . . . soon on Channel two,
"My Father the Rock". It will be all the rave,
(starring, as Erik the Rock, Handsome Dave).

Tenassity has her fine husband again,
and he never leaves from the house of his ken.
Children have father, and Muckus has friend.
They live ever happy. This is . . .

The End.

Glossary

Ade: Highly alcoholic, fermented lemon cider, traditional Ornian beverage believed to be good for the digestion.

Garlic: Very addictive bulbous root of the Dread Sea sage plant, known to cause hallucinations and halitosis.

Aker: Legendary wise man, court wit, and international practical joker . . . believed to be the origin of the term "wiseacre".

Algimemmitoes: Lak-Lustarian term for "light-footed oafish one".

Big Crum the Abused: Lak-Lustarian giant who had a very bad childhood which he took out on anyone and everyone he met.

Caloo and Callay: Literally translated as "I'm one happy nomad" and "Life is good again".

Careens: Desert land on the very edge of the midwestern demisphere of Orn (believed to have been the childhood sand-box of Festus, the God of Anvils) it was the setting for the famous book, *Warrior Klaus Stalvart of Vegotnofeers*.

Chorus: In traditional Ornian plays, the Great Talking Blackbirds have been employed as wandering minstrels and narrators.

Crontobasticon: Lak-Lustarian term for "cow of questionable breeding".

Dar moft: Green, large-nosed, pointy-headed people who primarily function as servants in Ornian society, they are believed to have been created by Dardalus Von Franken (the mighty Ornian Wizard).

Death: Santaklos, God of the Dead.

Death-bat: Carnivorous bat with a 30-foot wing span and sloppy dining habits.

Dweezil and Dutch: Mythic tale about a young couple who stroll through the woods and are hit by a stray thunderbolt from Moose, transforming them into two cans of Spam.

Erik the Blue: Greatest Lak-Lustarian hero to come out of the Ghast Garlic Wars alive. He was known for his fondness for the color blue and his abnormally small feet.

Eustashia: One of the favored lands of Hairless, the Goddess of Guts, located south of the Earlands of Headlia, along the canals into the throat of the Salivary Seas.

Fates: Three omnipresent forces in Ornian Mythology (usually depicted as women) known as The Good, The Bad, and The Ugly.

Gargle: A horrible she-beast that torments towns with her hideous sounds of excessive mouthwash gargling, it was believed that her horrible sounds would turn a man to styrofoam.

Ghast Garlic Wars: Wars between Toorelia (and allies) and the garlic traders of Oont to prevent the widespread garlic addiction that plagued the western regions about the Dread Sea.

Glin: Fishing village in the south of the Goolaphy Ocean

Great Snakey Twist: The most enormous of the crushing snakes on Orn, this beast was believed to have been created by Moose to unclog a plugged bath-tub in Olmpoo (the home of the Gods).

Hairless: The Goddess of Guts, best known for her support of warrior Heroes such as Thesod and Harry Clean

Harry Clean: Ancient hero from the town of Actin upon Myosin with the largest muscles ever to be seen on a human being. He was an undefeated warrior who eventually became the God of Muscles.

Hermafrodity: God of Gender Confusion.

Herman the Hess: Leader of the Evil Empire & Health Club of the North Central Midwestern lands of Pomerania. One Thousand and Two Pomeranian Knights was his infamous biography written by a quadroplegic slave, Abhul von Achtul the White.

Island of Rook: Small Island in the Goolaphy Ocean near the Crooked Straits, famed for very little.

Isle of Bad Rick: Obscure reference to a children's tale in which an evil emperor, Rick, tries to take over the world only to be stopped by a duck with a lisp and a stuttering pig.

Jack Fleet: Mythical hero whose speed was only surpassed by the winged feet of Quickslivver, the Messenger of the Gods.

King Muffler: After being accidentally turned into a cube of salt by Hairless (the Goddess of Guts), his ego became so great at being "chosen" that his neighbors dissolved him in water.

Kree: Ornian sailing vessel generally made of lead or some other heavy metal.

Lak-Lustar: Little known land on the easterly side of the Goolaphy Ocean. It was famous for its plain-ness that spawned the likes of Erik the Blue and Erik (The Mighty) Miteus.

Land seal: The common wheat-eating flippered dog, scourge of the wheat fields of Orn.

Makkie the Knife: Lak-Lustarian assassin and mercenary with a fondness for dirty fighting and big knives.

Max Walrus, hero of Glee: Large, obese (yet mighty) warrior of the Northern Icelands of Glee, famed for his Muttonchop whiskers and buck teeth.

Moose: The God of all Gods, a white-bearded, thunderbolt-throwing God who is easily angered.

Munchen: The ancient, hidden City of Lead.

Nuyork: An Ornian city existing only in mail order catalogs.

Oont: Harsh, rocky territory across the Dread Sea from Toorelia, known as the Land of the Garlic-eaters.

Purple Knight: Famous fictional villain and arch enemy of Klaus Stalvart, written by the first century writer, Glim the Weakling.

Queebs: Westernly city near Sturg (site of the Sturgeon war), it is the home of all Ornian wise men.

Quickslivver: The God of Messages and Travellers, also known as Burmese or Flash.

Shirley MacLaine: Ancient wise man and seer who proposed the theory of reincarnation, he is most famous for the phrase "Don't call me Shirley".

Skreet: Mythical hero whose enormous eyes covered nearly a third of his head, endowing him with incredible powers of vision.

Smoolies: Ornian currency, valued according to its metal composition (gold, lead, tin, copper), with lead being the most valuable.

Snow rhino: Large, hoofed beast with seven horns on the bridge of its nose. It lives in the ice caves of the northern winterlands of Fraica.

Speed-wining: The quickest way on Orn to make an intoxicating beverage is to add garlic . . . a process some refer to as "speed-wining".

Spengle, the wise God of Unbalanced Fights: Doesn't exist, fabricated by Yago in his attempts to fool Eric the Mighty.

Styrofoam: What? You don't know what styrofoam is?

Toorelia: Southernly country on the Dread Sea and the Goolaphy Ocean, famous for its serious and rigid society.

Underwhere: The underworld land of the dead, ruled by the Gods Playdough and Santaklos.

Warrior Klaus Stalvart: Hero warrior from the Glim the Weakling novels of the first century.

Wim the Unkind: Famed Lak-Lustarian warrior with a very bad attitude.

Zardoz: Mythical Warrior from the ancient Piglatin texts of Antislat.

Zorba the Geek: The ruler of ancient Geece in the land of Fredonia, famous for his powerful swordsmanship despite his frail, skinny body and his love for chess. Zorba is believed to be the origin of the term "geek".

Printed in the United States
201223BV00004B/1-30/A